Microaggressions in Ministry

Microaggressions in Ministry
Confronting the Hidden Violence
of Everyday Church

Cody J. Sanders
Angela Yarber

WESTMINSTER
JOHN KNOX PRESS
LOUISVILLE · KENTUCKY

© 2015 Cody J. Sanders and Angela Yarber

First Edition
Published by Westminster John Knox Press
Louisville, Kentucky

16 17 18 19 20 21 22 23 24—10 9 8 7 6 5 4 3 2

Chapter 6 is an adaption of an article that is republished with permission of Maney Publishing, from Cody J. Sanders, "Preaching Messages We Never Intended: LGBTQ-based Microaggressions in Classroom and Pulpit, *Theology & Sexuality* 19, no. 1 (2013): 21–35; permission conveyed through Copyright Clearance Center, Inc.

Book design by Sharon Adams
Cover design by Allison Taylor

Library of Congress Cataloging-in-Publication Data
Sanders, Cody J.
  Microaggressions in ministry : confronting the hidden violence of everyday church / Cody J. Sanders, Angela Yarber.
      pages cm
  ISBN 978-0-664-26057-6 (alk. paper)
  1. Violence--Religious aspects--Christianity. 2. Microaggressions. 3. Discrimination--Religious aspects--Christianity. 4. Church work. 5. Pastoral theology. I. Title.
  BT736.15.S26 2015
  253.08--dc23
                                                    2015031744

Most Westminster John Knox Press books are available at special quantity discounts when purchased in bulk by corporations, organizations, and special-interest groups. For more information, please e-mail SpecialSales@wjkbooks.com.

To my parents, Monty and René, and my siblings, Nick and Lacey
C. J. S.

To Riah, with hope
A. Y.

Contents

Acknowledgments

Mutual Acknowledgments

We are both profoundly grateful to Westminster John Knox Press and Robert Ratcliff for publishing this project. For the Alliance of Baptists, Baptist Peace Fellowship of North America, and the Association of Welcoming and Affirming Baptists, our denominational networks and homes, we are thankful. To the tremendous scholars and clergy who provided endorsements to help make this book a reality, we cannot thank you enough: Patrick S. Cheng, Miguel De La Torre, Gabriella Lettini, Derek Hicks, Mary Hunt, Rita Nakashima Brock, Kwok Pui Lan, and Emilie M. Townes. And for all the people who shared their stories with us, those myriad individuals who were vulnerable enough to speak about the way microaggressions have impacted their lives, we are honored to have worked with you. Because of anonymity, you remain nameless, but know how truly thankful we are to have witnessed your stories. Thank you for this.

Angela's Acknowledgments

In addition to those for whom we are both grateful, I am foremost thankful for Susan Parker, who worked side by side with me in a radical mutual ministry where we both learned a great deal together about the microaggressions in ministerial contexts. Susan first introduced me to the concepts of microaggressions; ministering alongside of her made the church more livable when it was difficult. I want to acknowledge the fabulous people at the Young Women Clergy Project, the Queer Young Clergy Women Project, and the Feminism and Religion blog for providing examples, both humorous and heart-felt, that reminded us all that we do not brave this ministry journey alone. I acknowledge the support and feedback of numerous colleagues and friends at Wake Forest University's Women's, Gender, and Sexuality Department and School of Divinity, along with other friends and colleagues from the Graduate Theological Union. These include Wendy, Melissa, Michelle, Angela, Sharon, Jen, Page, Kristin, Richard, Ryan, Mom, Dad, Carl, and Josh. Also, a true gift during this project has been writing with Cody; you are brilliant, dear friend, and writing with you has been a joy. I have learned much from you, and I appreciate that your skills in theory help to ground my storytelling. If someone had told me in seminary that ten years later the two of us would be out and proud and writing a book together, I don't know if I would have believed it. How grateful I am that our paths have crossed. It gives me hope for the church that you remain faithfully dedicated to its service. And I would be remiss if I did not acknowledge the support of my wife, Elizabeth, and our child, Riah. In the midst of academic and ministerial work, they make life more fun, silly, beautiful, and meaningful. Together, we hope that Riah may be able to grow up in a world where the church won't assault his soul for being different, but instead may celebrate humanity in all of its diversity.

Cody's Acknowledgements

I was first introduced to the concept of microaggressions in a pastoral theology doctoral seminar on race, gender, sexuality, and class taught by Nancy J. Ramsay at Brite Divinity School. Dr. Ramsay's careful attention to the complexities and intersections of race, gender, sexual orientation, and gender identity have profoundly shaped my own thinking and writing on these matters. Spending several years in the context of Brite Divinity School helped to expand my imagination and my hopefulness for how religious institutions can seriously and faithfully embody practices of justice in relation to human difference. I am also deeply appreciative of my coauthor, Angela, for your generosity with deadlines, your brilliant scholarship, and your caring friendship beyond the work on this book.

Introduction

1920: Women achieve the right to vote.
1954: The segregation of schools based on race is deemed
*   unconstitutional.*
2014: Thirty-three states offer legal same-sex marriage.

Many people—and many communities of faith—believe we live in a society where racism, sexism, and heterosexism are bigotries of the past. "Racism ended with the end of segregation," some claim. "Sexism is over because women can vote," others purport. "Gay people have all the same rights as straight people," still others believe. If you have picked up this book, we imagine that you likely do not cling to such beliefs. Many progressive Christians understand fully that racism, sexism, and heterosexism are alive and well. Even worse, such discrimination continues to thrive in churches, seminaries, and denominational bodies.

On the whole, most Christian communities are quick to condemn blatant discrimination based on race, gender, or sexuality. If a preacher were to utter a racial slur, claim that women have smaller brains than men, or say the "F-word" in reference to a gay person, most caring, thoughtful congregants would be quick to condemn such bigoted behavior. Open-minded, progressive persons of faith do not tolerate such outright discrimination. It's backward. It's close-minded. It's not politically correct. And it's not what Jesus would do.

Why is it, then, that countless women, persons of color, and LGBTQs face discriminatory treatment from the very faith communities that claim to nurture and affirm their souls? While blatant discrimination is often condemned, underhanded slights that assault the souls of oppressed groups still rage from the pulpit, the pew, the Sunday school class, the hymnal, the seminary curriculum, the ordination process, and in pastoral counseling. These everyday slights, insults, and invalidations are called microaggressions, and they

1

accost the spirits of women, persons of color, and LGBTQs on a regular basis in our churches, seminaries, and denominations. Because no one deserves to feel alienated by their faith community, assaulted by their seminary, or marginalized by their denomination; because discrimination is systemic; because oppression and marginalization are antithetical to the gospel; and because microaggressions are a theological issue, we have chosen to write this book. The hidden violence of everyday church can be captured in one word, and it is time that this word came into the conversations of faith communities. This word is *microaggressions*.

Cody's Reasons for Researching Microaggressions

I coauthored this book because I love the church. I've loved the church since I was a small child, first lured to the Christian tradition by the beauty of its music. The majestic sounds of the pipe organ and choirs communicated to me the deep significance of faith long before the words of sermons and Sunday school lessons made any sense. I loved it so much that I played church in my backyard in a small chapel my father and paternal grandfather built for me. Wearing a robe and stole my grandmother sewed for me, I officiated services alongside my maternal grandfather, whom I recruited to preach while I led the music. As a six-year-old, it seemed obvious to me that my love for the church would set the trajectory for my vocation. And the good people at the Southern Baptist church of my upbringing nurtured that sense of call with warm dedication.

Like musicians who move our hearts through delicate strains of music, like artists who use seemingly ordinary colors and brushstrokes to help us see the world in otherworldly light, like poets with a bent for stimulating our imaginations beyond mere words into ethereal spaces of imagination and insight, so too, churches are entrusted with a gift of elegant profundity. Our tradition, our ritual, our music, our sacred texts are comprised of words and images, narratives and embodied movements, sounds and senses that move us to dream new dreams when life has become a nightmare, to see new visions of the way things *ought* to be when the status quo threatens to undo us, to propel us beyond the constraints of the possible to undertake the impossible.

This is a dangerous gift. As a queer person, I've come to know this danger intimately. The beautiful profundity of the Christian tradition that shapes our imaginations, animates our embodied activity in the world, and directs the trajectory of our lives can have equally profound power to perform great harm. We need only look to the history of the Christian church to understand the power of our theological tradition to fuel violence on a grand scale and to legitimate unjust and oppressive social conditions such as slavery and the subjugation of women. As a queer person, I know the power of this profound theological tradition to perpetuate violence against the deepest sense of my own beingness—my soul—marginalizing my lived human experience.

This first-person knowledge of the power of theological language and ritual and communal space compels me to write about the potential of my own theological tradition to enact harm in the lives of racial minorities, women, and LGBTQ people through the hidden violence of microaggressions. In part, coauthoring this text gives voice to the ways I wish to hold accountable my own Christian tradition and the communities that formed me for the continued perpetration of this violence. But more compelling than my experiences as the *target* of microaggressions in ministerial contexts is my own *participation* in this hidden violence.

As a man, I am responsible for perpetuating patriarchal microaggressive behavior against women. As a white person (raised in the U.S. South), my consciousness is awash with racial prejudice, and my life is often lived in complicity with racially oppressive arrangements of power—no matter how much I consciously and intentionally attempt to live in accord with the aims of racial justice. As a cisgender man, my bodily, gendered self-understanding often leads me to overlook and invalidate the lived experience of transgender, intersex, and genderqueer people, rendering their experiences publicly invisible. As temporarily able-bodied, I am often complicit with microinvalidating environmental cues that ignore the needs of the disabled, making their lives unnecessarily difficult. In part, I coauthored this text as a way of taking responsibility for the times my many privileged embodiments intersect with my Christian theological commitments in ways that cause harm to others, most often unintentionally and outside of my conscious awareness.

To me, writing about microaggressions in the context of ministry is about helping individuals and churches take another step toward greater responsibility for the beautiful, dangerous gift contained in our theological discourses and ecclesial practices. Writing about microaggressions in ministry is also about providing language and a theoretical framework to the common experiences of racial minorities, women, and LGBTQ people who experience the hidden violence of everyday church in ways that white persons, men, straight, and cisgender people have great difficulty recognizing.

Ultimately, though, I write this book with my colleague Angela because I love the church. I was formed by the beautiful, dangerous gift of elegant profundity alive within the Christian theological tradition—its words, its rituals, and its music. I love the church, and I want to help communities of faith take greater responsibility for the continued cultivation of the beautiful, danger-ous, elegant, profound gift entrusted to us.

Angela's Reasons for Researching Microaggressions

"We're just worried that our children's program won't grow. I'm concerned parents won't want to bring their child to a church with a lesbian pastor and so many gay people," a deacon stated woefully.

"Isn't she pretty?" he said as he pinched my cheeks and introduced me to a prestigious male academic. "You'd never know she's smart."

Comments like these have been a regular occurrence in the fourteen years I have spent ministering in local churches and seminaries. As a queer woman, I knew that many elements of ministry blatantly excluded me on the assump-tion that my mere presence was a sin, an abomination. So I chose to affiliate myself with progressive, open-minded churches, seminaries, and denomi-national groups. All of these groups boldly proclaim to affirm women in ministry, and most are welcoming and affirming of LGBTQ persons. These organizations pride themselves on their openness. Yet I've found myself con-sistently feeling invalidated, excluded, and marginalized by some of the very people and organizations that claimed to be allies.

What makes dealing with these feelings so difficult is that the individuals who make statements similar to the comments listed above are most often good, thoughtful, moral people who never intend to be sexist, heterosexist, or exclusive. In fact, I would surmise that most would call themselves allies and say that they care about and work toward justice and inclusion for all people. Many even feel that the words they say are compliments.

Though I had experienced and witnessed such microaggressions throughout all of my ministerial tenure, I didn't have the language for grappling with them. I had never heard the term *microaggression*, and I constantly questioned my own feelings and experiences because the people invalidating and excluding me were ones I considered to be allies. My experiences of exclusion culmi-nated when my arrival at a church entailed having *two* out lesbians as head pastors. "Surely this will be a place where all will be welcomed, affirmed, and celebrated," I thought. Yet the microaggressive words and actions intensi-fied as good, thoughtful, progressive people acted out of their own privilege in ways that hurt, excluded, and marginalized an array of queer people, women, persons of color, and persons from different socioeconomic classes. "Did I hear him correctly?" "Am I being too sensitive?" "Surely she didn't mean that." These thoughts and questions constantly swirled through my mind.

As I tried to navigate this dissonance, I realized that other minorities within the congregation were experiencing similar things. I knew something was truly wrong when my physical health suffered and I began to feel depressed and anxious. I am very fortunate to typically be an incredibly healthy, upbeat person with a positive outlook. Yet as a pastor of this progressive congregation, I felt unwelcome, depressed, and anxious; I struggled with sleeping, eating, and low energy, and I couldn't figure out why. When a colleague shared a chapter of Derald Wing Sue's *Microaggressions in Everyday Life,* I felt as though he had read my mind, knew my heart, and named my struggles. I realized I was not alone, that my experiences were not invalid. I read everything I could find about microaggressions, realizing that I was not too sensitive and that many of the people perpetrating these microaggressions did so without malicious intent. If learning about the language, impact, and tools for addressing microaggressions could be such a balm for me, surely it could help other oppressed persons and groups in ministry.

I began talking with friends and colleagues of color, fellow women and queers, listening to their experiences and sharing the good news of microaggressions literature. Person after person—clergy, laity, seminarian, professor, denominational leader—virtually every individual from an underrepresented group had experienced some version of the everyday slights, insults, invalidations, and indignities Sue addresses. What made their stories so profound— and often heartbreaking—is that they didn't merely occur at work, in daily life, or at school. Rather these stories of exclusion, insult, and invalidation occurred within the walls of the church, packing theological weight onto an already painful experience.

In recovering from the ways in which microaggressively sexist and heterosexist behavior assaulted my own soul, I recognized a responsibility I have to help others grapple with these indignities. Moreover, studying microaggressions literature helped me to acknowledge when I have been a perpetrator of indignities, insults, and invalidations without even realizing it. Acting out of my own privilege as a white, educated, able-bodied person, I have been guilty of microaggression against others. Learning about microaggressions not only ushered in healing for my own assaulted soul, but it reminded me that—no matter how many antiracism trainings I attend and no matter how many books I've read about ability and privilege—I still have the capacity of marginalizing those who are not afforded the same privileges as me. Accordingly, the more I learn about microaggressions, the more I can alter my behaviors, attitudes, and words to be a better and more aware ally.

I cannot help but wonder if the churches in which I've served had prepared themselves better for what it might be like to have a lesbian pastor by learning about microaggressions, would it have been possible for all those insults, indignities, and invalidations to have never occurred? At the very least, we would have had the language and understanding for grappling with them. In partnering with Cody to write this book, it is my hope that we can help individuals suffering from microaggressive behaviors while also aiding churches, clergy, and seminaries in preventing this suffering from happening in the first place.

The church, in all its many forms, should be a place of welcome, affirmation, and inclusion, a place of grace where every person is respected, honored, and celebrated as a beloved child of God. I believe that such a church can exist. It can exist if we are willing to honestly examine our privileges and how our words and actions have the potential to assault the souls of minority persons. Let's create such a church.

Chapter Outline

Microaggressions in Ministry is divided into three sections. The first serves as an introduction to microaggressions. The second elaborates on the targets of microaggressions, highlighting race, gender, and sexual orientation and gender identity in separate chapters. The final section addresses microaggressions in ministerial practice: preaching and education, worship and spirituality, and care and counseling.

Chapter 1 reviews the current literature about microaggressions in the field of psychology. At the end of the chapter, we include definitions of terms from this field. We also include definitions of terms related to race, gender, and sexuality. This chapter is descriptive and historical, providing the language and a foundation for moving forward.

Insomuch as chapter 1 is descriptive, chapter 2 is constructive. Here we view the concept of microaggressions through the lens of religious and theological studies, claiming that the language and context of religion adds theological weight that further assails the souls of victims of microaggressions. We also provide examples of ways that the church excludes and maligns individuals with regard to race, gender, and sexuality without even realizing it.

Part II begins with chapter 3, which addresses microaggressions and race. Beginning with the stories of individuals who have experienced racial microaggressions in church, chapter 3 illustrates the way the church has excluded, invalidated, or maligned persons of color. Unpacking the ways in which the church's supposed colorblindness often upholds discriminatory norms that are not overtly racist, we provide tools for grappling with the "new racism" that faces churches in the United States.

Similarly, chapter 4 opens with the stories of women who have experienced gender microaggressions in church, illustrating the way the church has excluded, invalidated, or maligned women. Examining church polity and doctrine that intentionally exclude women is a first step. The second step explores the ways that churches claiming to include women in ordained ministry still exclude women's voices in underhanded ways. We provide tools for empowering women and grappling with microaggressive sexist behaviors still lingering within the church.

Concluding part II is chapter 5, which deals with microaggressions related to sexual orientation and gender identity. Beginning with the stories of individuals who have experienced microaggressions directed at sexual orientation or gender identity in church, chapter 5 illustrates the way the church has excluded, invalidated, or maligned the LGBTQ community. Examining church polity and doctrine that intentionally excludes the LGBTQ community is a first step. The second step explores the ways that open and affirming churches still have steps to take to become queer spaces, to subvert the heterosexist ideologies that linger within them. We provide tools for empowering LGBTQs and for grappling with lingering microaggressive heterosexist behaviors.

Part III takes the ways microaggressions impact women, persons of color, and sexual minorities and applies it to ministerial practice. Since many microaggressions are verbal, chapter 6 addresses the two areas of church ministry that deal most with the spoken and written word: preaching and education. First, we share stories of how preaching and religious education have excluded, invalidated, or maligned persons because of race, gender, or sexuality. Utilizing the constructive approach detailed in chapter 2, we provide tools for preachers and religious educators to use their words in ways that are affirming and liberating.

After addressing the explicit nature of spoken microaggressions in chapter 6, we address in chapter 7 the implicit theologies embedded in worship and spirituality. How are our architecture, art, music, and spiritual practices microaggressive? First, we share stories of how worship and spirituality have excluded, invalidated, or maligned persons because of race, gender, or sexuality. As in chapter 6, we provide tools that can be used in worship and spiritual practices so that all may be included and affirmed.

Drawing mostly upon the psychological field that first developed the concepts of microaggressions, we address in chapter 8 how this concept is employed in pastoral care and counseling. First, we share stories of how pastoral care and counseling have excluded, invalidated, or maligned persons because of race, gender, or sexuality. As always, we provide tools for pastoral counselors and clergy to use in pastoral care.

In the conclusion, we return to our personal reasons for writing this book. We also examine areas of growth needed in the research of microaggressions in ministry. Whose stories are not being told? Who has been left out of this text, such as persons experiencing microaggressions based on class, age, ability, or body type? How can we be more inclusive? These are questions we begin to address in the conclusion.

PART 1

Introduction to Microaggressions

Chapter 1

Introducing Microaggressions

Now that you know why we are interested in researching microaggressions and how such behavior is evident in the church, it's important to obtain a deeper knowledge of microaggressions. In order to understand how microaggressions relate to ministry, it is first imperative to grasp the implications of the social psychological research on microaggressions. We introduce it in two primary ways. First, we review the literature addressing microaggressions; this will help you achieve a deeper and more nuanced understanding of microaggressions. Second, we provide definitions for terms related to microaggressions and to terms related to race, gender, sexuality, and gender identity. When learning about a new topic, the jargon related to the field can sometimes feel overwhelming. Providing a list of terms from the outset will help you to better understand the rest of the book. Use these lists as a point of reference along the way.

Microaggressions in the Social Scientific Literature

We believe it is fair to assume that everyone engages in the communication of microaggressions. A great many of us are also the targets of microaggressions from time to time. Even so, for most, microaggression is an unknown concept.

The term *microaggression* was introduced to the scholarly literature by Chester Pierce in 1970.[1] In recent years, this potent concept has been reanimated by Columbia University professor of psychology and education Derald Wing Sue, a leading scholar in multicultural psychology and counseling.[2] While many overt forms of prejudicial and assaultive speech have diminished in recent decades, in a neoliberal society characterized by polite political correctness and a widespread denial that the oppressive dynamics of racism, sexism, heterosexism, and genderism are still at work, microaggression is a concept whose time has come. Microaggressions scholar Kevin Nadal argues that while "political correctness may seem positive in that it may lead to fewer instances of blatant discrimination (e.g., hate crimes; racial, sexist, and homophobic slurs), it may also result in the lack of awareness of one's unconscious or subconscious biases and unintentional behaviors."[3] The theory of microaggressions helps us to attend to those subconscious biases and unintentional prejudicial behaviors that we all inherit from a process of social conditioning that no amount of political correctness can cover.[4]

For this reason, microaggressions emerged in recent years as an influential theory within multicultural psychology and education. By Gilles Deleuze's account, "A theory is exactly like a box of tools. . . . It must be useful. It must function. . . . If no one uses it . . . then the theory is worthless."[5] Theologian Namsoon Kang furthers this Deleuzian notion, positing, "A discourse as a *tool* can effectively *function* only if it elaborates the *utopian* urge to think, judge, and act *otherwise*."[6] With this book, we attempt to combine discursive toolboxes—placing in conversation the social scientific conceptual tools of microaggressions with the arts of ministry and theological discourse. We do this with the hope of making the theory of microaggressions useful—*functional*—for ministers, congregations, and institutions of theological higher education by urging us all to think, judge, and act in ways that resist the harm perpetrated through these subtle communications of insult, invalidation, and injury based on embodiments of human difference.

What Are Microaggressions?

Sue defines microaggressions as "brief, everyday exchanges that send denigrating messages to certain individuals because of their group membership."[7] These exchanges can occur in verbal, behavioral, and environmental form and communicate subtle messages of hostility, degradation, or insult based on the target's race, gender, sexual orientation, gender identity, class, ability, ethnicity, national heritage, or religion.[8] It is vital to note that microaggressions derive their power to injure largely from their *invisibility* to perpetrators. In fact, perpetrators typically engage in microaggressive communication unintentionally and without conscious awareness.[9]

It is equally important to consider how microaggressions derive their power to harm through the citation of larger racist, sexist, heterosexist, and genderist/transphobic social discourses. Thus, microaggressive speech operates as a linguistic tool of oppressive force reflecting hegemonic "values,

biases, assumptions, and stereotypes that have been strongly culturally inculcated into our beliefs, attitudes, and behaviors."[10] Pedagogical theorist Henry
Giroux describes ideological hegemony as "those systems of practices,
meanings, and values which provide legitimacy to the dominant society's
institutional arrangements and interests."[11] Microaggressions covertly communicate the legitimacy of these oppressive beliefs, attitudes, and behaviors
through the three distinct forms of *insult*, *invalidation*, and *assault* based on
a target's race, gender, sexual orientation, or gender identity.

Microinsults

Microinsults communicate stereotypes, rudeness, and insensitivity toward an
embodiment of human difference, such as race, gender, sexual orientation,
or gender identity. Microinsults are subtly demeaning, snubbing the targeted
party through a comment or behavioral or environmental cue outside the conscious awareness of the perpetrator.[12]

A microinsult based on gender identity is experienced when Lisa, an MTF
(male-to-female) transgender person, fully presenting at church as female for
several years, experiences her Sunday school classmates continually slip-up
and address her with masculine pronouns (he/him/his) rather than with her
preferred female pronouns (she/her/hers). The classmates know better and
fully intend to use the female pronouns reflecting Lisa's gender identity, but
they unconsciously and inadvertently fail to do so, communicating insensitivity toward the embodiment of her transgender identity.

In another instance, a microinsult based on gender is perpetrated when
Deborah, an accountant with eighteen years of experience who is up for election as church treasurer, has her qualifications for the position questioned,
debated, and scrutinized by the congregation far more than any of her male
predecessors who were elected with a simple vote. Most of the congregants
believe they are just exercising their due diligence, but Deborah and several
other women in the congregation note the disparity between this election
process and those in the past. This microinsult is based on stereotypes of
women's roles as nurturing or caregiving rather than quantitative and business savvy.

Microinvalidations

In contrast to subtle insults, microinvalidations serve to deny the validity
of personal experiences for racial minorities, women, and LGBTQ persons
by imposing reality on these marginalized groups.[13] Microinvalidations

invalidate, negate, or exclude thoughts, feelings, and experiential realities of targeted parties. The potential for harm rests in the microinvalidation's ability to subtly define reality outside the conscious awareness or deliberate intention of those in the privileged majority groups in ways that uphold their unquestioned privilege while marginalizing others.

For example, Carlos—a third-generation U.S. citizen from New Jersey whose family emigrated to the United States from Colombia many years before Carlos was born—now attends collage at a small, predominantly white, Christian university in Texas. When he first became involved in campus ministry events, volunteering to pray and read Scripture, his peers often remarked how articulate he was and asked him how long he had been in the United States. While intended as compliments, these comments subtly invalidated his U.S. heritage and placed him in the position of "perpetual foreigner" in the eyes of his peers.[14]

An environmental microinvalidation based on race occurs when First Church—a historically white congregation in a now predominantly black and Latino/a area of the city—teaches its children's Sunday school classes using pictures and videos of Bible stories that portray biblical characters as white people. While the teachers do not notice the problem and certainly do not intend to communicate a racially invalidating message, the black and Latino/a children now calling this church their faith home are inundated for many years with the subtle message that the Bible is a book about white people.

Microassaults

Rather than the unintentionality and lack of perpetrator awareness characteristic of microinsults and microinvalidations, microassaults are most often conscious and deliberate and intend to communicate a demeaning attack or inflict harm based on a target's racial, gender, or sexual group identity.[15] These communications most resemble older forms of racism and sexism in their very deliberate and overt communication of denigration. Sue states that the conditions necessary for the communication of microassaults include the perpetrators either feeling some degree of anonymity, being in the presence of others who share their beliefs and attitudes and who will not hold them accountable for microassaultive communication, or losing emotional control and communicating prejudicial perspectives that they would normally keep to themselves.[16]

In an era of political correctness, when overt expressions of racism and sexism are deemed largely unacceptable in most churches and segments of society, microassaults in contexts of ministry are probably most common when targeting lesbian, gay, bisexual, and transgender people.[17] For example, from any number of pulpits throughout the country, an LGBTQ person might expect to hear LGBTQ persons denigrated as psychologically disordered or sinful because of their experience of sexuality or gender identity, expression of love, or formation of same-sex relationships. There is nothing subtle, unconscious, or unintentional about these communications, yet they do not always rise to the level of outright hate speech and so can be considered microassaults. While commonly experienced by LGBTQ people, microassaults are also common in the current immigration debates in the United States, denigrating the ethnic heritage and racial identities of persons from Central and South America. Additionally, in the wake of the U.S. "war on terror," persons of Middle Eastern descent or of Islamic faith are often targeted by microassaults that denigrate their ethnic heritage and/or promote Islamophobia.

The Experience of Perpetrators

While microaggressions are perpetrated every day by a multitude of people, most of us believe that we are generally good human beings who live moral lives and resist the prejudices that beset the society that surrounds us. It is surprising for many of us to learn that we communicate messages that are insulting, invalidating, and subtly denigrating to others based on their racial, gender, or sexual identities. That is because microaggressions, by definition, are perpetrated outside the conscious awareness of perpetrators, typically quite unintentionally, and often against the conscious self-perception we hold about ourselves as good, moral people. This understandably cultivates various forms of denial as a central experience for perpetrators of microaggressions.

Unawareness: "No, I Never Said That!"

Speech, actions, and environmental cues that target persons based on embodiments of difference such as racial identity, gender, or sexual orientation and gender identity are at times quite overt, but they garner the most power to damage and demean when they are covert and communicated outside the conscious awareness of well-intentioned perpetrators.[18] This is especially the case with the first two subtypes, microinsults and microinvalidations. Sue argues that a lack of perpetrator awareness surrounding their demeaning or denigrating communication is a central characteristic of both of these sub-types.[19] To a great extent, microaggressions are unconscious and seemingly automatic verbal or physical communications that occur outside of the aware-ness of the perpetrator, understandably leading to denial on confrontation.

This is certainly the case in the vignette with Lisa, the male-to-female transgender person whose Sunday school classmates continue to refer to her with masculine pronouns. Lisa's classmates know and love her and have been very supportive of her gradual process of transition. The continual slip-ups in using masculine pronouns are genuine mistakes that are so automatic that her classmates do not even realize they are communicating insensitivity to their friend. If confronted, some may even deny that they would do such a thing to insult Lisa by using masculine pronouns, and they quite legitimately may not recognize that they have done so! Nevertheless, the experience is painful to Lisa and makes her Sunday school class feel like an unsafe place.

Unintentionality: "Oh, You Know I Didn't Mean It like That!"

In the vast majority of cases, the perpetrator of a microaggression does not intend to be hurtful, demeaning, or insulting in any way. Since the speaker legitimately does not intend to communicate insulting or invalidating mes-sages, when confronted by a targeted party, it is easy for the perpetrator to say, "Oh, you know that's not how I meant it." Sue argues, "Being able to give legitimate-sounding reasons for actions taken protects the individual from realizing their unintentional discrimination; it allows people to maintain the illusion that they acted properly and without bias."[20] Again, we all usually see ourselves as good, moral people who eschew prejudice and oppression in our lives. But it is very difficult to purge ourselves of the prejudicial beliefs and oppressive worldviews inculcated within us by simply being raised in a social atmosphere where racist, sexist, heterosexist, and genderist attitudes circulate so widely.

Thus, the racially microinvalidating message may be quite unintentional in the vignette above in which First Church—a historically white congregation in a now predominantly black and Latino/a area of the city—teaches children Sunday school lessons using pictures and videos of Bible stories portraying biblical characters exclusively as white people. The pastors and lay leaders of the church are, in fact, quite dedicated to their community and have worked hard as a congregation to become a more welcoming space for their black and Latino/a neighbors. They've even lost many white members in recent years who didn't want to see their church "change in that way." Sandra, a new African American Sunday school teacher, decides to gently confront three of the longtime white teachers about these pictures and videos of all-white Bible characters. One Sunday after class, Sandra humorously says, "You know, if I didn't know any better, seeing these pictures and videos we use would make me think that the Bible was set in Sweden. Everyone's so white and blue-eyed." The white teachers respond by saying, "Sandra, you know they're just pictures. They're not meant to be racist. They're just all we have, and we really can't afford to replace them with new ones."

Self-Image Preservation: "But You Know I'm Not a Prejudiced Person!"

Believing ourselves to be generally good, moral, upstanding citizens who uphold the principles of democracy and live out a Christian ethic of love and justice, we can all be a little defensive when confronted with our own microaggressive communication. That nearly immediate, visceral reaction of defensiveness is perfectly understandable. But once we *know* about microaggressions and their power to harm, we have a responsibility to attend to the ways our unconscious, unintentional, nearly automatic communications can inadvertently perpetuate the racist, sexist, heterosexist, and genderist norms of our society in ways that harm our neighbors.

Defensiveness about our complicity in these microaggressive communications is a concern we must work to resolve within the context of our institutions and faith communities. When confronted, a perpetrator's denial can further the microaggressive experience, invalidating the targeted person's experience of reality by immediately shutting down discussion of the issue or shaming the targeted person for bringing it up in the first place. As Sue argues, "The ultimate denial is a denial that dominant group members profit from the isms of our society and a denial of personal responsibility to take action."[21]

Deborah, the church treasurer-elect from the example above, told her male pastor how hurt she was that it seemed her fellow congregants didn't trust her qualifications to be treasurer. Deborah believed they were reluctant to elect her because she was a woman, despite her many years of experience as a CPA and her dedicated service to the congregation. Her pastor immediately responded, "Now Deborah, I can't believe you would say that! You know women are treated as equals in this church! Folks just wanted to make sure they were electing a qualified person to this important position. The process would have been the same for a male candidate."

In this statement, the pastor perpetuated Deborah's microaggressive experience by denying that her perception of the situation had any validity. Even more invalidating was the pastor's seeming reluctance to recognize that no matter the intention of the congregation in this specific instance, his church belongs to a denomination that struggles over women's leadership, with very few congregations being led by female pastors. While the pastor's internal defensive reaction is perfectly understandable, with the tools of microaggressions theory, he may become more willing to acknowledge with Deborah that her interpretation of this experience is valid, as there is a long history of sexist leadership norms within the denomination that it struggles to overcome. In an open discussion with Deborah about the difficulties of the congregation and wider denomination in overcoming historic stereotypes about and prejudices against women, the pastor may be more open to learning from Deborah the lessons that will help him cultivate a climate of greater gender equity within the congregation.[22] At the very least, this small change in the pastor's response would carefully guard against perpetuating the hurtful microaggressive experience Deborah has already encountered.

The Experience of Targets

Ambiguity: "Did That Really Just Happen?"

Microaggressions are filled with double meanings—overt messages at odds with hidden ones. Thus, messages intended to be positive, or at the very least innocuous, are attended by a subtly derogatory message entirely unintended by the speaker. These unintended messages derive their power to harm from citations of larger racist, sexist, or LGBTQ-denigrating social and theological discourses.[23] For example, a middle-aged, white, professional-class gay man is told by a parishioner of his congregation, "I'm so glad that you're the example of a gay man this church has. You're just so normal, and that will help people become more accepting of gay people." Intending to be complimentary, the microinsult contained in this message communicates the subtle message that gay people in general are abnormal and generally beyond the realm of what would be acceptable to the congregation.

The subtlety of microaggressions leaves in question the possibility that the experience of the targeted person may simply be a misreading of a situation or evidence of oversensitivity on the part of the recipient. Sue terms this phenomenon *attributional ambiguity* and describes it as one of the most damaging aspects of microaggressive communications. He argues that the attributional ambiguity of microaggressions "depletes psychological energy by diverting attention away from the surrounding environment in an attempt to interpret the motive and meaning of the person's actions." Thus, when confronted by a microaggression, the targeted person must first discern the truth of the microaggressive experience while protecting oneself from further insults and invalidations.[24]

In the above experience of Carlos, a third-generation U.S. citizen from New Jersey whose family immigrated to the United States from Colombia many years before Carlos was born, he must discern whether or not his campus ministry peers mean to communicate anything about his racial and ethnic heritage with their comments about his "articulate" way of speaking. If he asks them about these statements, he may open himself to accusations of being overly sensitive or paranoid. Nadal describes this as the catch-22 of responding, by which he means that microaggressions are often so ambiguous that targets may question whether or not their experience of the microaggression really occurred or whether they are just being paranoid.[25] After targeted persons have come to some resolution about whether or not their perceptions are accurate, Sue says that they must try to ascertain what actions, if any, should be taken.[26] If they do choose to respond to perpetrators, they may open themselves up to further microaggressions or even overt aggression. If they do not respond, they may feel a deep sense of regret or inauthenticity.[27]

Action: "What Should I Do Now?"

Nadal describes the internal dialogue a targeted person often experiences when deciding whether and how to take action in responding: "What will happen if I confront this person? How will this affect my relationship with her or him? Will my physical or psychological safety be compromised if I say something? If I don't confront the person, how will I feel, and how will it affect me in the future?"[28] While the internal risks/benefits may lead a targeted person to believe that the situation is not safe to make a confrontation, the effects of not allowing one's beliefs and feelings to be known can be psychologically, emotionally, and spiritually harmful, inducing feelings of cowardice, beliefs that one has sold out, and feelings related to a loss of integrity.[29]

Sandra judged the potential of harming the relationship with her fellow Sunday school teachers to be fairly low, as they all get along well and the church has an overall atmosphere of attention to concerns of racial justice. So she decided to defuse the potential tension around the situation by couching her confrontation in a little humor. Though her coteachers denied the problematic nature of the pictures and videos of all-white Bible characters, Sandra felt good about having brought the subject to their attention and believed there to be potential for raising the subject again in the future.

Lisa has depended so much on this Sunday school class for their love and support during her process of gender transition. She leaned on them when her own family rejected her, and she spends so much of her time with members of this class that she judges the risk too great to confront them. She simply sits through each class and social gathering, bracing herself for the inevitable slip-ups of masculine pronoun usage. The experience is now depleting her psychological and emotional energy and distracting her from the spiritual growth she once felt she gained in this class. But because she's afraid of losing these relationships, confronting her classmates just seems too risky.

Impact: "Why Is This Affecting Me So Much?"

Sue argues, "The internal struggle with microaggressions can fester and eat away at the integrity of the person for long periods of time."[30] The recipient may experience feelings of sadness, anger, frustration, discomfort, lack of safety, embarrassment, shame, and a host of other affective responses.[31] Over time, the chronic, continual nature of microaggressions can wear down the targeted individuals, leading to feelings of exhaustion through the persistent experience of a hostile and invalidating climate that demeans one's racial, gender, or sexual identity and subtly demands that one comply with dominant experiences and expression of reality.[32]

While there are a variety of means for coping with and resisting microaggressions (a goal of this book is to increase those means), coping and resisting are not always effective in changing the environment in which microaggressions are occurring. When coping is unsuccessful or ineffective, the targeted person may experience the troubling emotions of depression, guilt, apathy, anxiety, and anger alongside a lowered sense of well-being, increased physiological reactivity, and the biological consequences of stress.[33] In the next chapter, we will address in depth the potential for theological language and symbols to intensify the violence perpetrated by microaggressive communication.

Carlos attempted to endure the microaggressive experiences he encountered from his predominantly white campus ministry peers. When the immigration debates in Texas began to become a lively source of discussion on campus, many of his peers assumed that Carlos could provide them with a firsthand perspective and often asked him at meals or in class to comment on the experience of an immigrant. Carlos, who has never even traveled outside of the United States, tried to explain that all Latinos/as do not share a common experience, but this rarely seemed to get through to them. Moving from a racially and ethnically diverse school, church, and community in

New Jersey to a mostly white Christian university in Texas, Carlos knew his everyday experience would be vastly different. What he didn't expect was that his peers would treat him as a perpetual foreigner in his own country. Carlos eventually decided to stop confronting his peers, as the confrontations rarely seemed effective to bring about change. Carlos began experiencing a persistent mixture of sadness and anger and eventually dropped out of his campus ministry groups without explanation, becoming more withdrawn and feeling isolated on his small college campus.

The Goals of Addressing Microaggressions

Given that microaggressions are communicated in ways that are largely unintentional and outside the conscious awareness of perpetrators with great potential for denial, Sue asks, "How do we make the invisible visible? How do we reach people so that they can become aware of their biases? How do we make people see the harm perpetrated against socially devalued groups in our society?"[34] These are important guiding questions for our exploration of microaggressions in ministry. Our goals in helping ministers, churches, and other religious institutions to address microaggressions are threefold.

First, we aim to increase microaggressions *awareness* by making the invisible visible. If microaggressions education in congregations and faith institutions takes hold, there is potential to increase the awareness of perpetrators and lessen the experience of ambiguity among targets so that microaggressions can be addressed more openly when they occur. We aim to raise readers' awareness of the many subtle and nearly automatic ways our speech and actions are shaped by the racism, sexism, heterosexism, and transphobia/genderism still circulating in wider society. We hope that this will mean fewer slights, insults, and invalidations will slip by our conscious notice and that when they inevitably do, recipients of those microaggressive communications will have the conceptual tools necessary to name the experiences in ways that may bring about change.

Second, we want to provide ministers, congregations, and institutions tools for microaggressions *assessment.* By evaluating the prevalence and potential of microaggressions to cause harm within religious contexts, these environments can become more just, welcoming spaces. Beyond internal assessment, however, we hope that churches and other religious institutions will become spaces where persons are equipped with strategies for coping with and resisting microaggressions *outside* church walls. With these enhanced tools, they can deal with the insulting, invalidating, and assaultive messages affecting themselves and their friends and neighbors.

Third, we hope to provide tools for *action* in order to bring about substantial change. This begins with the simple task of bringing microaggressions into conscious, intentional conversation. The goal is not to make us too paranoid to speak but to help us become aware that we *will* perpetrate microaggressions and that we need strategies and tools in order to grapple honestly with this reality, to decrease the occurrence of microaggressions, and to ameliorate their potential to harm within our churches and wider communities. As homiletics scholar Christine M. Smith states, "To speak honestly about our individual lives and the conditions of the human family is a powerful act of resistance in a world committed to the denial of truth."[35] By addressing each ministerial context in its specificity—preaching and education, worship and spirituality, pastoral care and counseling—we hope to provide readers with these practical tools for honestly engaging microaggressive experience with the aims of healing and resistance.

A Note Regarding Terms

Recognizing and properly addressing microaggressions is hard. For many readers the very concept of microaggressions is new, even though the reality of them is not. Compounding the difficulty is the fact that microaggressions are not all the same; they are, rather, a complex mix of attitudes, perspectives, and behaviors. To deal with this complexity, those who study microaggressions and the related issues of race, gender, and sexuality have come up with certain specialized terms—for example, the distinction between microaggression and microassault. We will, at times, draw on this vocabulary. If you encounter terms with which you are unfamiliar, please consult the glossaries toward the end of the book.

Chapter 2

Assailing the Soul

Microaggressions in Ministry

Ministerial Microaggressions in Action

Everyone Is Welcome

*T*errance, a black college student, had attended worship at an African Methodist Episcopal (AME) Church every Sunday with his family, where his mother sang in the gospel choir. Like many students, Terrance spent his first few years of college sleeping in on Sundays and then catching up on his studies rather than attending church. As his senior year approached, Terrance began to reevaluate his life and question what he wanted to do for a career. Warm memories of his childhood church, partnered with his roommate's invitation to attend worship, helped him decide that bolstering his spiritual life was probably a good step in discerning how to shape his life after college.

Terrance's roommate assured him that his church welcomed everyone, sang good music, and had a really cool pastor. Terrance set his alarm for Sunday morning, put on his best church clothes—dress slacks, a crisp tie, and vest—and began humming some of his favorite songs from his church's gospel choir. With his Bible in hand, Terrance waited for his roommate to finish getting ready so they could leave for worship together.

Glancing over at his buddy clad in jeans and a jersey, Terrance questioned his outfit. Sensing Terrance's unease, his roommate assured him that at this church, everyone just comes as they are because everyone is welcome. This didn't resonate with Terrance's childhood experiences of putting on one's Sunday best for God, but he trusted his roommate, confident that church should be a place where everyone is welcome.

When they arrived at church, everyone was very friendly to Terrance, welcoming him with a handshake or hug. Though he felt that everyone was kind, Terrance couldn't help but feel at odds. Immediately, he noticed that he was the only black person in the sanctuary. Though he saw one or two other persons of color, no one else was dressed in attire as formal as his own. When worship began, Terrance's discomfort intensified. The songs of his home church were nowhere to be found in the service. In fact, every one of the songs sung by the congregation, as solos, by the band, or during the prelude or postlude were composed by or written by white men. Terrance always thought of himself as thoroughly "churched," familiar with the stories of the Bible and capable of singing all the gospel hymns and spirituals by heart, but he had never sung any of the songs at his roommate's church.

After worship, Terrance's roommate asked him what he thought of church: "Isn't everyone so friendly and cool?" While Terrance agreed that everyone was, indeed, really friendly, he couldn't help but feel like he didn't belong. Instead of feeling inspired to examine his next steps in life, Terrance felt bad for not liking the church as much as his roommate did, but he couldn't quite discern why. "If everyone is welcome, why did I feel so left out?" Terrance wondered.

What Does It Mean to Affirm?

Diane was in her final semester of seminary and was in the process of interviewing for jobs in churches. After college, she had a ten-year career as an attorney and was often praised for her public speaking skills and professionalism. In seminary, Diane discovered that her gift for public speaking translated into a gift for preaching. She never felt more alive than when she preached. Acknowledging a tremendous sense of call to the pulpit, Diane did an internship at a church that gave her the rare opportunity to preach once a month. Overjoyed, Diane hoped this experience would aid her in applying for ministry positions.

Though she had excellent grades, myriad recommendations praising her skillful preaching, and wonderful interview skills, Diane was dismayed that she was only offered one interview for a position that involved regular preaching. She received countless offers to interview for positions in children's and youth ministry, and she even got a few responses from churches that said how much they affirmed women in ministry but that they "weren't quite ready for a woman as senior pastor."

Holding firmly to her calling, Diane interviewed with the one church that was interested in her. It was a small congregation forty miles outside of the closest large town, with about thirty-five in attendance during worship on an average Sunday. Though the church was small and couldn't pay very well, the members prided themselves in affirming both men and women in ministry. When Diane arrived for her interview, she discovered that there were no women on the search committee. All the men on the committee were nice and complimentary, telling her numerous times that she was well spoken and very pretty. The committee decided to ask some icebreaker questions in order to get the conversation going. Rather than asking about her ministry or preaching experience, the first question the committee posed to Diane was whether she was married and had children. Diane felt uncomfortable with this question—especially after being told how pretty she was—but she wasn't sure whether her discomfort stemmed from her corporate law background, where such questions were not legally permitted.

The time came in the interview for Diane to ask questions of the committee. She asked, "How many women have been ministers at your church in the past?" The committee chuckled and responded, "We affirm women in ministry, but all of our pastors have been men. We just hired who was best for the job, and that's the way it turned out."

Though her interview experience didn't quite feel right, Diane was delighted to be invited to the church to preach in order to be voted on by the congregation as its next pastor. She researched, wrote, and polished her sermon and was ready when the Sunday arrived. As worship began, the chair of the search committee introduced Diane to the congregation by saying, "We've heard she's the best woman preacher in town!" While Diane appreciated his compliment, she couldn't help but feel uneasy. The congregation stood to sing the opening hymn, "Good Christian Men, Rejoice." Diane stood, wondering if anyone would notice whether she replaced the word "men" with "folk" while she sang. As she approached the pulpit to preach a few minutes later, she didn't feel enlivened but wondered whether this church really understood what it means to affirm women in ministry.

Inclusion and Invalidation

Collette and her wife, Jane, decided that the birth of their first child was the perfect time to find a church. Though Collette was raised in a church that believed homosexuality was a sin, she had heard that there were some churches that include and celebrate LGBTQ people. So after perusing several church websites, the couple found a local church that advertised itself as "welcoming and affirming." Collette was so excited that she wanted to attend worship and Sunday school as soon as possible, especially since Christmas was just around the corner.

Even though Jane had to work that Sunday, Collette and their baby set off for worship, eager to see what a "welcoming and affirming" church would be like. As they pulled into the parking lot, Collette took a deep breath, remembering the many times her childhood pastor hollered about how homosexuals were an abomination from the pulpit. As she unhooked her son from his car seat, she couldn't help but smile at the thought of being able to worship without being condemned.

The church's website advertised a nursery for babies and a Sunday school class for young couples, so Collette carried her son in the direction of the nursery. When she arrived, she was greeted with enthusiasm as nursery workers fawned over her adorable baby. They handed her a form to fill out in case of emergencies and asked, "Where is Daddy today?" Luckily, Collette was used to hearing this question and quickly responded, "Oh, my wife had to work this morning, so we decided it would just be the two of us." "Great! We're a welcoming and affirming church, so we're glad to have a baby with two moms." Reassured, Collette handed over her child and sat down to fill out the nursery form. In the space for "mother," Collette listed herself and then crossed out the space for "father" and wrote "other mother," listing Jane's name and contact information.

When Collette arrived at the class for young couples, she was greeted warmly once again. She looked around the room and saw six other couples, all male-female. The teacher asked, "Is your husband working today, or are you looking for the young singles class?" Collette sighed and repeated what she had told the nursery worker: "My wife had to work this morning." "Wait a second," a class member chimed in jovially. "I didn't think gay people could get married in our state." Collette began her introduction to the class by having to explain the difference between having a marriage ceremony and receiving legal rights via civil marriage.

As class ended and Collette made her way to the sanctuary, she felt torn. On the one hand, she knew she was at a "welcoming and affirming" church. No one called her a sinner or an abomination, but something didn't feel quite right. As worship began, Collette learned that it was the second Sunday of Advent. The Scripture lesson proclaimed that God would make "the crooked straight." A hymn that coincided with the lesson was next, and the congregation began to sing about God making the "crooked straight." Again, Collette just didn't feel right. While the church proudly proclaimed that it welcomed and affirmed people and families like hers, she couldn't help but feel that the classes and the worship ignored her difference and tried to make her a little more straight. Instead of leaving feeling welcome, she left feeling invalidated.

Dangerous Binaries

Brad is a pre-op transgender man. When he told his parents that his gender identity didn't match the gender he was assigned at birth and that he wanted to begin hormones to aid in transitioning into who he fully was, his parents told him, "Our daughter is welcome in this house. If you are no longer our daughter, you are no longer our child." A fight ensued as Brad's parents insisted that "she" was merely a tomboy, and Brad's belongings were placed in a trash bag on the front lawn. Brad crashed on a friend's couch for a few nights while searching for a shelter or permanent residence. The entire experience left him feeling very alone and unwanted.

Fortunately, Brad lived in a town large enough to have an LGBTQ center, which had a list of resources for young people, including a few churches that are open and affirming. Brad decided to attend, hopeful that the church might provide a new sense of family, welcome, and love. When Brad arrived at church on Sunday morning, an usher greeted him kindly and offered him a bulletin. Brad was grateful for the warm welcome and asked the usher to point him in the direction of the bathroom before worship began. The usher responded, "The lady's room is just around the corner, ma'am." Brad immediately felt horrible, not knowing whether to tell the usher that he's a trans man and feeling ashamed that he didn't "pass" in the way he presented himself. Wanting to avoid an awkward conversation in the first few minutes at the new church, Brad hung his head and made his way to the women's restroom. As he was washing his hands, a teenage girl gave him a little poke in the ribs and said, "Uhmm, I think you got the bathrooms mixed up. This one is for girls! The men's room is across the hall." Apparently, Brad did pass in her eyes.

Brad questioned whether he should even stay for worship, since he'd already had two awkward encounters. Intent on finding a family who loved him, he stayed. The pastor stood behind the pulpit and offered a warm greeting, "Brothers and sisters, welcome to God's house, a place where all are welcome, whether you're male or female, black or white, rich or poor, gay or straight." The pastor continued by offering a special welcome to visitors and inviting them to fill out an information card in their bulletins. Though Brad didn't feel comfortable as a brother *or* sister, he opted to fill out the visitor card. His discomfort intensified on the very first line: "Circle *Mr., Ms.,* or *Mrs.*" Brad didn't circle anything and instead listed his chosen name: Brad. "Check *male* or *female*," the card continued. Brad's eyes filled with tears just as the music minister invited the congregation to stand and sing. "Let's begin with everyone singing verse one, the ladies singing verse two, and the men singing verse three," the music minister told the congregation with enthusiasm.

Not knowing what part to sing, which bathroom to use, or what box to check, Brad left worship before the opening hymn was even finished. He knew it was a welcoming and affirming church and everyone was nice enough, but the entire experience left him feeling very alone and unwanted.

Microaggressions in Ministry and Everyday Life: What's the Difference?

While microaggressions may be an entirely new concept for many readers, chapter 1's explanation of microaggressions as subtle verbal or nonverbal slights, insults, or denigrating environmental cues targeting persons based on their racial, gender, or sexual identities should paint a clear picture of their power to harm individuals in the course of everyday life. But for those involved in religious contexts—whether the ministry of local congregations, religious nonprofit organizations, or theological higher education—understanding the power of microaggressions to harm individuals requires moving beyond the point where the social science literature leaves off. We must turn to other resources to understand the potential for microaggressions fueled by religious and theological language and symbols to harm differently and, in many cases, much more intensely.

The differences between microaggressions occurring in ministry settings versus microaggressions experienced anywhere else in society centers on the *language*, *symbols*, *metaphors*, and *narratives* in these varied settings. Microaggressions that operate with the force of religion take on an intensified ability to harm. The qualitative difference between microaggressions in everyday life and microaggressions in ministry might be likened to the difference between the potential for injury if stabbed with a pocketknife versus the potential for injury if stabbed with a sword. Both hold potential for bodily harm, but one is able to penetrate more deeply and harm more extensively. For microaggressions, however, our focus is on the penetrating power of words, not weapons.

The task of this chapter is to expand on the work that Sue and other social scientists have offered in addressing the destructive potential of microaggressions in everyday life by turning our attention to instances of microaggressions in ministry. We will pay careful attention to the differences between religious language and everyday speech. If at any level we acknowledge the power of religious language and symbols to promote healing and the flourishing of life, we must also carefully understand their converse potential to injure and diminish the livability of life. Imagining language and symbols as tools, we ask: What can we do with religious or theological language and symbols that we can't necessarily do with other linguistic and symbolic tools? How do the tools of religious language and symbols work on people in both creative and destructive ways? And how can we ensure that we are using our linguistic and symbolic tools as carefully as possible and for the purposes we intend to use them—namely, the promotion of healing and the flourishing of life—rather than for injury and the diminishment of life? It is to these questions that we now turn.

The Power of Religious Language and Symbols

Recall Sue's definition of microaggressions from the first chapter: "brief, everyday exchanges that send denigrating messages to certain individuals because of their group membership."[1] These exchanges take place in the form of words, gestures, and environmental cues. The greatest power of microaggressions to wound, as mentioned in chapter 1, is their inherent ambiguity. Did the speaker really mean that? Did I even hear that correctly? Is this really the message the speaker intended to communicate, or am I reading too much into it? Should I confront the speaker or just let it go?

The ultimate ambiguity of a microaggression exists in trying to discern whether or not this small instance of language is a citation of a much larger unit of language—that is, the narratives and discourses that attempt to define who we are as human beings in relation to one another. The power of a microaggression is in its subtle ability to cite a larger social discourse of oppression—whether of racism, sexism, heterosexism, or transphobia. Lucy Atkinson Rose, a professor of preaching, argues that "all language, including the language of faith, is inevitably biased and limited, historically conditioned, and inseparable from the sins of each generation and each community of users."[2] Microaggressions occurring in ministry must always be understood in light of the sins of each generation—in our case, the sins of racism, sexism, heterosexism, and transphobia. It is from these societal sins of prejudice and hatred and the many ways we enshrine them into institutions and social practices that microaggressions take their cue. These larger oppressive social discourses are "cited"—kind of like an unspoken footnote—by microaggressions, and they give the microaggressions the power to wound deeply.

For example, in the case of Diane, there were several clear instances of microaggressions targeting Diane as a woman. Interview questions addressing Diane's marital status before her ministerial credentials and experience and comments about her appearance by the all-male search committee would be considered microaggressions in any job interview. For Diane, however, the experience may have been even more invalidating because she was a woman attempting to enter the role of pastor in a congregation and denomination with a long history of excluding women from access to this position of spiritual leadership. Such microaggressions gain greater power to injure, insult, and invalidate through their tacit citation of historic Christian discourses that interpret Scripture in ways that suggest women occupy a subjugated status. When this male-privileging discourse showed up again in the hymns sung in morning worship, Diane may well have wondered if this congregation had taken the necessary steps to truly affirm women in ministry or if she could continue to expect these types of microaggressions if she became the pastor.

The language and symbols we use in the practices of ministry—in preaching, worship, religious education, and pastoral care—may either uphold the social sins of our generation and therefore give theological credence to racist, sexist, heterosexist, and transphobic messages and practices or actively challenge and resist the power of these destructive forces.[3] Religious language and symbols not only have the capacity to uphold these social sins, but in three very specific ways, religious language and symbols have the capacity to *intensify* the strength of these oppressive social discourses. This occurs in the three interrelated capacities of religious language and symbols to tell us who we are as individuals, to place us in relation to others, and to place us in relation to an ultimate reality. As noted in chapter 1, many of the most prevalent ways we perpetuate these social sins are not in overt racist, sexist, heterosexist, or transphobic diatribes, but in subtle, often unintentional "citations" of these discourses that we may not even recognize we are communicating, as in the cases represented in the vignettes above. It is to these microaggressive capacities that we now turn, giving attention to three important features of religious language and symbols.

Religious Language and Symbols Tell Us Who We Are

Human beings are linguistic beings. While other species have systems of communication with various degrees of complexity, intricate and robust systems of language and symbols for communication seem to be the most unique feature of the human species. It is strange, then, that we so often teach our children to disregard the importance of this distinct human feature with platitudes such as "Sticks and stones can break my bones, but words can never hurt me." Words can hurt. Indeed, words can destroy.

It is out of the realization of language's destructive potential that philosopher Judith Butler asks, "Could language injure us if we were not, in some sense, linguistic beings, beings who require language in order to be?"[4] Butler suggests that our vulnerability to the destructive potential of language is a direct result of our being "constituted" by language. By this she means that language—words, stories, narratives—informs us of who we are as human beings, bringing into being our deepest sense of selfhood and weaving our multifaceted identities out of these linguistic and narratival threads.

If a friend asked you to explain who you are, you would most likely use language to do so. You might tell the story of your upbringing (of course, there is no "*the* story" of your upbringing—you would tell a particular *version* of the story suited to your particular audience). You might list attributes about yourself. "I'm a compassionate person," for example. "Why do you say so?" your friend might ask. In response, you would have a story or two to tell about how you came to know yourself as a compassionate person. "Who else has seen you this way in your past? Why is this attribute so important to you?" your friend might continue, requiring another story.

In more institutional settings, you might be required to say something about yourself by checking boxes on a form: age, sex, race, nationality, religion, etc. In those instances, you would be constrained by the language provided to describe who you are as a person. Oftentimes, the language we would prefer to use isn't even represented on the form.

If you were in your congregation or faith community and were asked to describe yourself using the religious language and symbols of your tradition, what might you say? Perhaps you would say something about what your faith tradition teaches is of ultimate significance about ourselves as human beings. Perhaps you would say that you are made in the image of God, that you are a person of sacred worth, or that you feel called to live your life by certain practices and principles. The religious language systems within which we live provide a great deal of the material we use in piecing together our self-understandings.

Our sense of self is constituted by language in all of its forms—from the personal stories we tell about ourselves and the stories others tell about us to the narratives that attend the social designations of race, ethnicity, class, sexuality, gender, age, and so forth that we are constantly required to claim as descriptive of ourselves. Religious language, however, attempts to reach beyond the personal and the social. As linguistic creatures—constantly understanding ourselves through the means of language, story, and symbol—we have often defined one aspect of our uniqueness that deserves particular attention in this discussion of microaggressions: the soul. Whatever you believe about the soul—whether you think of it as an eternal essence of our personhood that will live on into eternity, or whether you simply see it as a metaphor for our deepest sense of who we are as human beings, our self's sense of core identity—the language of "soul" has a long history.[5] But more importantly, it has *depth*—it is language that attempts to get at something central to our personhood.

For our discussion, you need not believe anything in particular about the soul to recognize that religious language and symbols attempt to move beyond personal and social descriptors to say something of our sense of the depth of our core as humans. Indeed, many of us find our ways of understanding who we are as human beings profoundly influenced by religious upbringings and the language worlds of our faith communities. It is this ability of religious language and symbols to speak to us about the nature of our humanity and our core sense of being that is important in understanding the damaging potential of microaggressions in ministry.

Religious Language and Symbols Place Us in Relation to Others

As much as human beings are linguistic beings, we are also "other-seeking" agents—directing our language, behavior, and activity toward others and, in turn, being constantly related to in language, behavior, and activity *by* others.[6] *We are who we are only in relation to other people in our lives.* While we have noted the ways that language works in the construction of the self (i.e., socially constructing the individual's self-understanding), we now turn to language at work on the level of the social (i.e., bringing individuals into the meaningful awareness of others in society). As philosopher Charles Taylor says, "One is a self among other selves."[7]

It is helpful to recognize that the constitution of one's self-understanding is sometimes at odds with the way one is brought into social being through the language and narratives that proliferate *about* one's being. This is often the case with the social discourses cited by microaggressions. For example, the not-so-distant portrayal in history of gay and lesbian people as sick or mentally ill or as deviant criminals through discourses of psychiatry or jurisprudence was at odds with the way gay and lesbian people experienced themselves and their own sexual and affectional orientations. This prompted activist movements to reform those denigrating social discourses and bring to the foreground previously subjugated language and narratives about the realities of lesbian and gay lives.

As this example illustrates, the language, symbols, and stories that put us in relationship with others are, of course, not entirely under our command. We do not individually create the language we use to talk about ourselves in relation to others. We live within a social space where this language, these symbols and stories, precede us. This is especially true in the case of life within a faith tradition that is millennia old. Similarly to the discourses of psychiatry and jurisprudence in the example above, in many ways, religious language and symbols provide materials for the creation of the social space that we all inhabit. And it is in this construction of social spaces that our religious language and symbols can place us in relation to others in some rather dangerous ways.

Pastoral theologian James Farris points to two aspects of religious language that cause grave problems when we understand ourselves in relation to others. The first is dualistic ways of understanding creation. (The second is the use of hierarchical understandings of nature, which we will return to later.) Farris argues that "dualistic ways of viewing creation have allowed, and continue to allow, the denigration or negation of those not defined as useful, valuable, viable, and so forth by the dominant group or culture."[8] Dualistic thinking divides reality into black-and-white categories. A few common examples shape the way we categorize people: male/female, straight/gay, young/old, wealthy/poor. When dualistic thinking comes to shape our theology, it produces strong divisions such as good/evil, holy/profane, heaven/earth, and light/dark. In each of these examples, the dominant social mindset privileges the first word in each pair, ascribing a high level of value to it while ascribing less value or even scorn for the second term. The simplistic, black-and-white lines that are drawn between conceptions of good and evil make it all too easy to apply a dualistic mentality to our binary divisions between groups of people.

Let's consider the story of Brad in the opening of this chapter to discover what dualisms or binary divisions those instances of microaggressions might have been building on. Brad's experience hinged on the binary division between male and female from the very beginning of his experience with the welcoming and affirming congregation. As a female-to-male transgender person, Brad identified as a man but had not yet been able to access the medical treatments he desired for a process transition (e.g., hormone therapies, surgery). Nevertheless, he was presenting as a man in his day-to-day life. This in-between space is a delicate one for Brad, as some look at him and see a woman (the usher), and others look at him and see a man (the girl in the bathroom). The inaccessibility of a gender-neutral bathroom and the forced gender choice (circle *Mr., Ms.,* or *Mrs.;* check *male* or *female*) on the welcome forms are prime examples of environmental microaggressions that invalidated Brad's gender experience. Add to that the further binary divisions between male and female upheld in worship in the pastor's welcome and the hymn's division between men and women, and the message is clear: There is no place for you here — in our building, in our worship, in our awareness — even though this is probably the last thing anyone in this congregation wished to communicate to Brad. While these experiences could occur anywhere, there is a citation of theological proportions here, as Scripture passages such as the Genesis creation narratives have been widely used to denigrate transgender, intersex, and genderqueer persons and to invalidate their experience of nonbinary or gender-nonconforming lives by claiming a "natural" or "God-ordained" order to creation based on gender binaries (male/female). It is likely that some of this theological weight was behind the decision of Brad's parents to kick him out of his home, too, as it is in many similar instances of transgender homelessness.

Beyond the ability for religious language and symbols to tell us who we are as individuals and to place us in relation to others, these linguistic and symbolic tools have a third function that provides even greater injurious strength to microaggressions occurring in ministerial settings.

Religious Language and Symbols Place Us in Relation to an Ultimate Reality

As Allen Carter points out, "Religion intensifies some things better left unintensified."[9] This intensifying effect of religion is certainly operating in the case of many of the "sins of each generation" mentioned by Rose above. Legitimizing our social sins of racism, sexism, heterosexism, and transphobia by setting them within religious terms strengthens the power of these identity-constructing narratives to penetrate our hearts, minds, and souls and justifies the ways that social relations are arranged to support these denigrating ideologies. Religious language has even been used to fuel and legitimate acts of racist, sexist, heterosexist, or transphobic physical violence. Remember, religious language and symbols seek to say something of consequence about our sense of the self's coreness, or soul, and they serve to place us in relation to one another. But they also serve to place us in relation to an ultimate reality. Often, though not always, we term this ultimate reality "God."

At this point, it is important to note Farris's second characteristic of Western European spirituality, which he sees as the construction of a "transcendent ontology." Put simply, theological interpretations drawing on a transcendent ontology construct a "natural" hierarchy of value and worth that serve to reinforce dominant/submissive, privileged/targeted patterns of relationship based on dualistic understandings of the world (e.g., male/female, straight/ gay, young/old, white/black, wealthy/poor). Recall that the first term in each of these binary pairs is the privileged term and thus finds its way to a "higher" position on the hierarchy that is constructed.

Theologian Gordon Kaufman describes the arrangement of power often communicated in our theological language in this way: "Power and knowledge are ordered so as to move from their source on high down through the hierarchical layers of society, each higher rank having authority over those below and the whole structure legitimated by the divine king ruling over all."[10] Farris makes clear the connection of these hierarchically arranged binary divisions to violence, both physical violence and microaggressive speech: "The fundamentally violent dynamic is that we label the other side as ontologically less valuable, therefore more easily disposed of, different, therefore 'other,' and continue hierarchical power based oppressive relationships."[11]

When another person or group of persons is symbolized as inferior, unnatural, or deviant with the language of transcendent hierarchy and portrayed through dualistic theological constructions (e.g., good/evil, natural/unnatural, normal/abnormal, light/dark), an understanding of the world and its "proper" arrangement is imposed that theologically serves to support a constellation of social relations of authority, power, domination, and violence. This theological dynamic then gives rise to—or at the very least gives credence to—the social sins of racism, sexism, heterosexism, and transphobia, further ingraining them into our understandings of self/other and defining the relations that exist between us.

Kaufman summarizes the trouble that results when hierarchical and dualistic theological constructions conveyed through language, symbol, and narrative interface with social arrangements of power and privilege:

> Those who know (or believe they know) what God wills, have inside information on the ultimate ordering activity in the universe, and feel authorized, therefore, to carry out whatever course of action seems required to implement this. To "serve God" is to try with all the resources at one's disposal to impose this order on whoever or whatever appears disobedient or rebellious.[12]

Not only does one side of the binary division become validated as inherently more valuable than the other, but the value and worth of a particular group are also made to seem legitimate by the group's placement on a theological hierarchy. In this hierarchy, value and worth are not distributed equally. God is at the top, straight white men with capital come soon after, and all those less valued by society (women, children, LGBT people, the poor, racial minorities, etc.) fall somewhere down below.[13]

The power of religious language and symbols to intensify the social sins of racial, gender, and sexual prejudice can be seen in a few brief examples. Christian slaveholders often appealed to Scripture passages—such as "the mark of Cain" in Genesis or Paul's admonition for slaves to be obedient to masters—to promote slavery as a God-ordained way of life. Similarly, many churches continue to interpret Ephesians 5:22–24 literally—"Wives, submit to your husbands as to the Lord"—in order to make women subservient in households, in church leadership, and in every endeavor outside the home. Finally, many antigay churches have claimed that "God made Adam and Eve, not Adam and Steve" to support heterosexual relationships and demonize same-gender relationships.

Recall from the vignette of Collette at the beginning of this chapter that as she and her child pulled into the parking lot, she took a deep breath, remembering the many times her childhood pastor had hollered from the pulpit about how homosexuals were an abomination. While she was entering an avowedly welcoming and affirming congregation, the residue of these anti-LGBT invectives lingered in Collette's consciousness. These anti-gay messages that are still very prevalent in wider society serve as the theological material that is tacitly cited in Collette's experience inside the church. The power of these theological messages is invoked first when she is continually asked about her husband—a question that presumes that man-woman-children is the normative configuration of relationship—and later when she encounters the microinsult from her Sunday school classmate who immediately questions the validity of her relational status with her wife. While Collette recognizes that she hasn't outright been called an abomination by anyone, as might have occurred in her childhood church, the theological hierarchy that was drawn on in her childhood to teach God's disdain for the "homosexual" continues to be inadvertently cited by these innocent and sometimes ambiguous invalidations of her experience as a lesbian mother in a welcoming and affirming congregation.

How Microaggressions in Ministry Cause Harm

To summarize, the potential for harm caused by microaggressions in ministerial settings is threefold. First, by serving to tell us who we are as human beings, microaggressions occurring in ministerial contexts, deriving rhetorical power from religious language and symbols, cut to the depths of who we believe we are as individuals.

For those who become targets of microaggressions in religious contexts, this can mean continued, repetitive insult, invalidation, and denigration to the deepest sense of self, or soul. Didier Eribon describes the damaging effects of insult and hatred, much of which can be communicated most "effectively" through microaggressive speech, for gay persons:

> The long-term effects of insult and hatred . . . write themselves into the body; they act by way of your own submission to the injunction that they carry, your own consent to the order they enforce—that your personality and your desires must remain hidden, that the line must be toed. They command you always to act "as if." They necessitate a permanent effort to ensure that none of your emotions, feelings, or desires are ever revealed.[14]

While Eribon is addressing the realities of gay people, this is an apt description of the long-term effects of microaggressions when also targeting persons based on race, gender, or gender identity. The persistent microaggressive messages write themselves into the body, shaping possibilities for life in deleterious ways, failing to promote healing and flourishing and, instead, dealing injury and the diminishment of life.

Second, by placing us in relation to others in society—often through upholding binary divisions between certain types of people—microaggressions that play off of religious language and symbols serve to legitimate and perpetuate oppressive social relations. They serve to subtly instill in our collective consciousness the second-class citizenship of certain persons in certain spaces. Microaggressions in ministerial settings—which derive their power of intensification from religious and spiritual language—concretize oppressive social relations between people by making binary divisions seem natural or even divinely ordained, and thus much more difficult to challenge.

Third, by setting understandings of individuals and social relations within an ultimate context—often by constructing a transcendent hierarchy of value and worth—microaggressions that draw on religious language and symbols invoke notions of what is natural or divinely sanctioned to bolster their subtly invalidating, insulting, or denigrating messages. They recruit God—or, more accurately, the *symbol* "God"—as a participant in the perpetuation of prejudice, oppressive relations, and violence, thus giving religious strength to the sins of each generation that diminish livability for racial minorities, women, and lesbian, gay, bisexual, and transgender people.

Ministerial Microaggressions in Action:
Possible Responses or Solutions

There is no simple solution to microaggressive behavior. It is not as though we can provide churches and religious institutions with a formula they can implement in order never to commit a microaggression directed at someone's race, gender, sexual orientation, or gender identity. Based on the constructive framework we have provided above, however, there are some steps churches can take to nourish and sustain the souls of persons of color, women, and LGBTQs rather than assailing them. Below are a few responses to each of the vignettes that opened the chapter. They are not so much solutions as ideas for preventing these microaggressive behaviors from happening again, aimed at helping churches become places where all are truly celebrated and honored.

Everyone Is Welcome

It would be easy for a white person to read Terrance's story and assume that his discomfort had little to do with race and everything to do with worship style. Couldn't anyone go to a church with a different style of worship or code of dress and feel a bit excluded? While this may be true, it is all too easy for white churchgoers to forget about the privilege they bring into worship. They may feel welcome and included because when they look around the sanctuary, virtually everyone looks like them, whether or not they dress like them. The person preaching and the leaders in worship all have white skin. The music, liturgies, and art included in worship are all created by other white people. Additionally, white people haven't had to deal with race-related fatigue during the days and moments leading up to worship.

Terrance felt as though he didn't belong, not because the worship style was different or because he was dressed nicer than almost everyone else in church, but because there was nothing in worship that reflected his histories, cultures, or traditions. One response that could make a difference is for worship planners to balance worship leadership by inviting a variety of different people to lead so that no one race, ethnicity, gender, age, or sexual orientation is overly represented. A second response is to examine whose traditions are represented in music, liturgy, and art. Was every song composed by a white man? Does the language of hymns or litanies employ binaries that equate darkness with evil and lightness with what is good, pure, and holy? Is every image of Jesus and other holy figures white? A final response is to examine the use of the phrase "all are welcome." Of course, all Christians claim that all are welcome. We believe this because we want it to be true. But churches need to be careful in claiming that all are welcome when all are not represented in worship. If the subliminal message is "You're welcome here as long as you dress, behave, and believe like me," that is a faulty sense of welcome.

While Terrance's roommate had good intentions in inviting him to worship and may have genuinely felt that Terrance would have a friendly and "cool" experience, it would have been more thoughtful to consider how Terrance might feel entering a church where he was the only black man present and virtually the only person of color. Perhaps Terrance's roommate could have engaged Terrance in an honest and thoughtful conversation about what kind of music his church sings, how people dress, and what the current demographics of the congregation are.

Part of what made Terrance's experience so difficult is not that the church or his roommate did anything overtly racist—quite the contrary. Everyone was kind, friendly, and welcoming. Terrance's roommate even told him that his church was a place where everyone *should* feel welcome. Terrance felt at odds because he experienced friendliness and heard the claim of welcome on the one hand but also experienced a deep sense of exclusion on the other. The entire experience left him questioning his feelings about attending church, and he almost felt guilty that he did not share his roommate's warm response to worship.

While some microaggressions, particularly microassaults, can cut sharply and deeply by ostensibly demonstrating that one doesn't belong, other microaggressions, such as the ones Terrance experienced, are much more difficult to navigate and understand. The goal for churches and religious institutions is to create spaces where people like Terrance don't have to feel torn and wonder whether the church is sincere in its proclamation that all are welcome.

What Does It Mean to Affirm?

Diane's story, much like Terrance's, is all too common. Countless churches claim to affirm men and women equally in ministry, but when examining the polity, leadership, and workload of these same churches, it is clear that women do not hold an equal amount of power or leadership as men. What might this little church do differently to avoid treating Diane and other women with microaggressively sexist behaviors?

First, in the same way that it is important for churches to be honest about what they mean when they claim that "all are welcome" (as we saw in Terrance's story), it's also important for churches to be honest about how they put their beliefs about equality into practice. Diane could have prepared herself differently for her interview had she been told that while the church truly wants to affirm women equally, women have never served in leadership and so the church is trying to learn how to be more affirming. A large part of what made Diane so uncomfortable is that she understood she was interviewing at a church that affirmed women in ministry. She was not prepared to experience otherwise because she thought she was entering a safe and affirming place.

What elements of her encounter led Diane to feel so uncomfortable? The first trigger was that there were no other women represented on the search committee. The committee's first question did not address her skills for the position but instead pried into her personal life. With a background as an attorney, Diane was aware that questions such as that—and more importantly, the responses to these questions—should not impact whether or not one is hired for a job. Beginning with a personal question made Diane wonder whether her response might sway the committee. If she said she wasn't married, would the committee see her as too desirable to be a minister? If she said she had young children, would the committee worry that she wasn't capable of taking care of her children and her congregation? These are concerns women are forced to deal with on a regular basis in balancing work and personal life.

Additionally, the committee continued to make comments about Diane's personal appearance. Even when offered as compliments, remarks about a woman's appearance often contribute to her feeling objectified, as though her looks are more important than her skills. Similarly, when the committee chair introduced Diane to the congregation, he described her as "the best woman preacher in town." Again, this was probably intended to be a compliment, but by qualifying her preaching ability by naming her gender, Diane's inferiority as a woman was implied. She's not the best preacher, but the best *woman* preacher. It is as though women are not on the same playing field as men.

Finally, exclusive and sexist language was used in worship. Since dictionaries and style guides have for decades deemed it academically archaic to use exclusive language when describing humanity, suffice it to say that this church is a bit behind the times. Instead, hymns, liturgies, and all spoken words in worship could employ either gender-neutral language for God and humanity or inclusive language that evokes particulars.

Inclusion and Invalidation

One may also wonder why Collette felt so invalidated at an open and affirming church. Does not the church explicitly say that it welcomes LGBTQs? Didn't the nursery worker rejoice at having a child with two mothers in the nursery? Like the churches in Terrance and Diane's stories, the congregation Collette visited did not do anything to actively discriminate. It was a church that truly believed it was welcoming and affirming everyone. In order to understand why Collette left the church feeling as though her life and relationship had been invalidated, let's step into her shoes for a moment.

If everywhere you looked—from books to movies, television to magazines, government legislation to popular culture—you rarely saw families that looked like yours, and your family did not even receive the same legal rights as most families, and you decided to attend a church that claimed to celebrate your family, how would it feel when the first person you met assumed that your family was like the majority? "Is your husband at work today?" might not seem like a cutting question, but Collette had to validate and name her relationship with her wife in virtually every encounter she had. The nursery worker, the form for emergency contacts, and the Sunday school teacher assumed heteronormativity, thus forcing Collette into a category where she did not belong. Such experiences could be avoided if churches asked about "other parent," "spouse," or "partner" rather than "mother" and "father." Even better, churches could not assume that a parent necessarily has a significant other, thus avoiding marginalizing single people.

After Collette's sexuality and familial relationship was invalidated, her experience worsened when a straight member of the Sunday school class revealed no knowledge of the discriminatory civil and legal issues that Collette's family has to navigate on a daily basis. By no means are we implying that every church needs to know every detail of all discriminatory laws, but if a congregation is going to claim to be open and affirming to LGBTQs, that entails knowing the legal discrimination they face in the community. ~~Diane~~ *Collette* might have felt differently—affirmed and validated—if someone in the Sunday school class had responded, "It's just not right that you can't get married legally in our state. That's why our church has organized a letter-writing campaign to our congressperson." Not only would ~~Diane~~ have felt like her relationship was validated, but she would not have had to take on the role of teacher by explaining the way she is marginalized in daily life.

Finally, while it may seem to be making a "mountain out of a molehill," as some critics of microaggressions have claimed, hearing Scripture and hymnody that claims that "God will make the crooked straight" was the last straw for Collette. One could argue that the text should not be interpreted to have anything to do with straightness in sexuality. This is true. But remember that Collette—like many LGBTQs—was raised in a church that told her that she was going to burn in hell, that she was an abomination, and that she needed to be straight in order to be loved by God. Though most straight people would never think that such Scripture or hymns are trying to convert LGBTQs into being heterosexual, this exclusive and binary language can strike a painful chord in the hearts of many LGBTQs. It certainly did for ~~Diane.~~ Colette.

Dangerous Binaries

Since transgender and genderqueer individuals make up such a small and marginalized part of the population, the dangers and discrimination they face on a regular basis are rarely considered by most churches, even ones that consider themselves open and affirming. Such was the case in Brad's story.

As in every other story, no one at the church Brad visited was intentionally malicious and discriminatory. Many of the encounters Brad experienced could be described as "no big deal," "a misunderstanding," or "not the church's intention." To see how Brad may have felt, step out of Collette's shoes and into his for a moment.

Your family has just disowned you, as is the case for countless transgender people.[15] You are looking for a new way to create family, you've found a church that claims to celebrate and honor people like you, and the first thing that happens when you walk through the doors and need to find a restroom is that you are faced with discrimination and exclusion. Choosing which bathroom to use is no small task for transgender persons. Each time some transgender people need to use the facilities, that person may have to choose whether to risk being yelled at in one or beat up in another. This is a daily reality. Churches can make an inclusive stance by simply having gender-neutral bathrooms. No one has to choose. No one has to be forced into a category where they don't belong.

Being forced to choose a binary category was the other issue that assailed Brad's soul. Not only did the restrooms limit him to "male" or "female," but so did the visitor's card. Similarly, the pastor's welcome appeared to include everyone: male and female, black and white, rich and poor, gay and straight. But this greeting, combined with calling the congregation "brothers and sisters," appealed to dualistic binaries where not everyone fits. Brad felt as though he had to choose this or that, brother or sister, male or female in order to belong. And even if Brad had been comfortable choosing one, he was reminded that his choice—brother, male—was not the way he was perceived by the usher who directed him to the women's room.

When the music minister divided the congregation into parts by inviting women and men to sing separately, Brad could take it no more. Instead of dividing the singing of verses between "men and women," the music minister could have divided them between vocal parts—sopranos and altos on verse 1 and tenors and basses on verse 2—making no assumptions as to the gendered nature of these vocal parts. But this was not the case in church that morning. Imagine knowing in your heart that you are a man, striving to dress and live accordingly, and wanting to sing the men's part, but knowing that your voice is too high because you have not yet begun hormone treatments. Not wanting to face the part of himself that his parents would still accept but that Brad knew was not his true self, he chose to leave church before the hymn concluded.

Conclusion

Terrance, Diane, Collette, and Brad each have a unique story that is illustrative of a larger issue. Like countless persons of color, women, and sexual minorities, their souls have been assaulted by microaggressions in the church. It is important to note that none of their experiences were at churches that are blatantly and unapologetically racist, sexist, heterosexist, or transphobic. On the contrary, each attended a congregation that prided itself in being inclusive and welcoming of everyone.

Terrance likely would not have chosen to attend a church if the pastor was a member of the KKK because Terrance would have known he wasn't safe or wanted there. Diane likely would not have interviewed at a church that claims women should be submissive to husbands and should not hold leadership positions in church because Diane would have known she wasn't safe or wanted there. Collette likely would not have chosen to attend another church that preached that homosexuality is an abomination because Collette would have known that she wasn't safe or wanted there. And Brad likely would not have chosen to visit a church that protests the funerals of transgender persons because Brad would have known he wasn't safe or wanted there. In each of these hypothetical situations, Terrance, Diane, Collette, and Brad would know that they are not safe, and they would know how to posture and protect their souls from the damaging impacts of blatant racism, sexism, heterosexism, and transphobia.

What makes dealing with microaggressions so difficult—for both the perpetrator and the victim—is their often unintentional ambiguity. Unfortunately, progressive churches that pride themselves on inclusion are sometimes the worst at owning and addressing the ways their privileges blind them to such damaging attacks to the souls of persons of color, women, and

LGBTQs. For many of these progressive, welcoming, and inclusive congregations, engaging in dialogue and the intentional reform of ministerial
practices in relation to the realities of microaggressions is the logical and
necessary next step in the process of widening the scope of inclusion, welcome, affirmation, and belonging.

PART 2

The Targets of
Microaggressions

Chapter 3

Microaggressions and Race

Ministerial Microaggressions in Action

Race, Theology, and Pastoral Authority

*H*arold is a forty-three-year-old African American man in a yearlong clinical pastoral education (CPE)[1] residency at a midsize religiously affiliated hospital in the midwestern United States. Soon after starting his residency, Harold began noticing that the medical and nursing staff and the administration of the hospital were predominantly—overwhelmingly—white. Harold also has five peers in the CPE residency, all of whom are white, and his male supervisor is a white Midwesterner. The only black and Latino/a people Harold sees on a regular basis are kitchen staff, transport workers, and environmental services staff.

When the CPE residents share their verbatim case presentations with one another, Harold often draws on black theologians such as James Cone and Anthony Pinn—formative figures in his own theological training—to develop theological understandings of his own autobiography, as well as the suffering experienced by his patients. During one of these presentations, a white peer confronted Harold on his choice of theological sources, asking, "Why do you always go to these black liberation theologians? Can't you use some regular theology like Barth or Tillich in your presentations from time to time? I think it would really strengthen your work." When Harold told his peer that that statement troubled him because it seemed to put black theologians in a lesser category than the white theologians the peer had named, his peer replied, "Harold, please don't think I'm racist. I'm not saying this because you're black. I don't even see you as a black man. I just see you as a human being and a child of God. I'm only trying to help."

During the five months Harold has served as a chaplain at the hospital, he has also noticed the tendency of the medical and nursing staff on his assigned floors to ignore his contributions to patient presentations during clinical rounds, to dismiss the input he voices, and to rarely, if ever, ask him directly for his perspectives on patient care. Harold brought this experience to his peer group and discovered that this feeling of marginality in the clinical team is not shared among his peers, many of whom are regularly called on by nursing staff for consultation in patient care and all of whom feel well integrated into the clinical team. Harold wonders to himself if his pastoral authority and professional role on the clinical team are not being recognized and respected because of his race.

Harold senses his CPE experience wearing on him emotionally and spiritually, and he is uncertain how to process these experiences. He brought these marginalizing experiences up during his individual supervision, but his CPE supervisor simply said, "Harold, racism isn't a problem at this hospital. This is a very tolerant place to work. Racism isn't a problem here like it is in the South where you grew up. I think you are just coming on too strongly in your relationship to staff and your peers, and that is a turnoff to people." He encouraged Harold to heed his CPE peer's advice to decrease his dependence on black liberation theologians, as these perspectives can be very intimidating and alienating to his white peers, who have come to see Harold as angry and overly confrontational.

A Case of Mistaken Identity?

Victoria is a twenty-eight-year-old Latina woman with two young children, three and six years old. Her husband, a white man named Clint, works every Sunday morning managing a retail store in town. Victoria and Clint would like to raise their two children in church, so Victoria begins taking them to a congregation close to their suburban home after researching the congregation online and discovering that it has a robust children's ministry with many children the age of her own.

Victoria arrives at the church on her first Sunday with the children. She finds the beautifully decorated children's ministry building and takes her two boys to the welcome desk to find their classrooms. The white woman at the children's welcome center greets Victoria and asks her to supply some information for the two boys to keep on file at the desk. "Can you give me their parents' names?" the woman asks. "Their father's name is Clint Smith," Victoria responds, and before she has the opportunity to go any further, the woman asks, "And are you their nanny?" "No, I am their mother, Victoria

Smith," she replies. "Oh, I'm so sorry," the woman replies. "The boys don't look Hispanic, and I just assumed. I'm so sorry." Victoria is used to this type of question, as the children do resemble their father in complexion and have much lighter hair than Victoria, but she is annoyed that the woman thinks she is a domestic worker rather than the children's mother.

After dropping the children off in their classrooms, Victoria makes her way to the sanctuary. A few kind, older white men greet her at the back of the sanctuary. Recognizing that she is a visitor, they help her find a seat. They show her to a pew four rows from the back of the long sanctuary. Victoria notices that there are many other empty seats closer to the front. She decides to move closer to the front so that she can see better.

During the passing of the peace, a white woman sitting in the pew in front of Victoria introduces herself with a warm smile. The woman then says, "You know, you might be interested to know that we have a Spanish-speaking service here at the church at one o'clock in the fellowship hall. It's an exciting ministry!" Victoria responds, "Thanks, but I don't speak Spanish very well." "Oh, how long have you been here?" the woman replies. "All my life," says Victoria. "I grew up about forty miles west of here." Victoria decides to skip the remainder of the passing of the peace and takes her seat for the remainder of the service.

As Victoria settles in for the Scripture reading, she hears the words of John 12:46: "I have come as light into the world, so that everyone who believes in me should not remain in the darkness." She then notices the title of the sermon: "Casting Out the Darkness." Though she knows this isn't the intention of the Scripture or the sermon title, she can't help but be reminded of the ways that her darker skin seem to make her an outcast in the sea of white bodies that fill the sanctuary that morning.

White Privilege

Many of our discussions about race and racism in ministerial and theological contexts begin only when a person of color enters our ecclesial or institutional space. We begin many of these discussions with the lived realities of racial minority group members, looking at instances of prejudice, injustice, and systemic oppression in their lives. But there is another important place to start discussion: addressing the lived experience of white people and the often-overlooked reality of white privilege. This starting point recognizes that racism is not only about a system of disadvantage based on race, whereby racial minorities experience interpersonal prejudice, systemic injustice, and violence based on their racial group membership. Racism is also a system of *advantage* for white people in a society structured by a legacy of racial injustice that privileges white racial identity over all others.[2]

In order to understand the importance of foregrounding whiteness in a discussion of racial microaggressions, we must challenge dominant cultural messages that strive to portray whiteness as neutral or as a *lack* of racial identity. When we do not recognize "white" as a racial category, we mistakenly believe that all of the cultural and social norms that attend whiteness are simply the given norms and that everything else represents difference (or even deviation[3]) from that presumed white norm. We must learn what theologian Eleazar Fernandez states so clearly: "Racism affects every aspect of our lives, all the time, wherever we are, whether people of color are present or not."[4] Fernandez points out that whiteness is not an absence of color or racial identity. Instead, he states, "White is a color, and white people are as colorful as the so-called people of color."[5] White people must, therefore, recognize the ways our bodies are racial bodies and come to understand the unearned advantages that attend our white racial identity. Understanding white privilege will assist us in making sense of the power of microaggressions to legitimate and perpetuate dynamics of racial prejudice.

In her famed essay "White Privilege: Unpacking the Invisible Knapsack," Peggy McIntosh images these unearned privileges as "an invisible weightless knapsack of special provisions, maps, passports, codebooks, visas, clothes, tools and blank checks" that white people can cash in on everyday without ever having to recognize that they are doing so.[6] These privileges are built in to our everyday experience as white people, whereby we are assured that our white values and norms are the values and norms undergirding most of our institutions—including white-dominated religious institutions.

Sue lists white cultural values and norms such as the belief in a just world where good things happen to good people and bad things happen to bad people, a prime value placed on individualism over collectivism, an emphasis on competition over cooperation, the separation of thinking from emotions, prizing verbal communication over nonverbal, and a belief that hard work will always lead to success.[7] If you are white, all of these probably seem quite commonsensical, as simply descriptive of the way things work in the world. If you're reading this from another racial perspective, you are well familiar with these norms and values, as you've had to live by them in many areas of your life, but you may be less sold on their "commonsensical" nature. It is white people's *presumed normativity* of these norms and values—the assumption that they are simply neutral values unaffected by racial identity—that perpetuates the unquestioned, unexamined nature of white privilege.

While there are many helpful resources for learning more about white privilege, for our discussion, it is the unexamined nature of white privilege that is most important. This is, in large part, why race-based microaggressions often fly under the radar of consciousness for white perpetrators, who do not recognize the many ways their own speech and actions privilege white values, norms, and ways of being in the world while, at the very same time, unintentionally diminishing, insulting, or invalidating other racial identities.

Lest we forget that we are engaging in a *theological* examination of microaggressions, it is important to name the diminishment of life for marginalized parties as an expression of *evil*. Womanist theologian and ethicist Emilie Townes explains the way that evil is culturally produced:

> The cultural production of evil can and does entrap many if not most of us. We often operate out of structurally determined limits that do, at points, offer some creativity and autonomy—but these are controlled and managed by hegemonic forces. . . . It only creates an austere marginal space that can lull many of us into a false but oh-so-deadly consciousness that contours our imaginations.[8]

Indeed, the deadly contouring of our imaginations and inculcation of a false consciousness not only serves to perpetuate microaggressive harm to racial minorities but also serves to diminish the lives of white people too.

White privilege intersects in a variety of complex ways with other markers of human difference (e.g., gender, class, sexual orientation, gender identity). As Frances Kendall, a scholar and organizational consultant on white privilege, states, "All of us who are white have white privilege, although the extent to which we have it varies depending on our gender, sexual orientation, socioeconomic status, age, physical ability, size and weight, and the like."[9] These intersectional identities are not simply additive, such that adding one minority status to another increases the likelihood of microaggressive violence in a formulaic equation of oppression. Rather, they are interactive and shape our experience of privilege and targeting in complex ways.

But for those interested in addressing multiple expressions of oppression and marginalization, another intersection is important to recognize as well, as Kendall argues:

> Believing that race is "not my issue" and being members of one or more groups that also experience systemic discrimination, we use the privilege of emotionally and psychologically removing ourselves from the "white" group, which we see as composed either of racists or of white, straight, healthy males. For those of us who are white and women and/or lesbian or gay, our experience of being excluded from the mainstream hides us

from the fact that we still benefit from our skin color. By seeing ourselves as removed from the privileged group, we are all the more oblivious to our silencing of people of color.[10]

Thus, it is important for those of us who are white but who also identify with another marginalized group based on our gender, sexual orientation, gender identity, ability, class, and so forth to understand our own complicity in race-based oppression and the perpetration of racial microaggressions, no matter the other ways we may experience microaggressive violence.

Being overly dismissive of another's experience of racial microaggressions because of our own experience of marginalization is itself a microinvalidating communication. When what we are really trying to do in these cases is empathize and increase our understanding of another's experience, it is helpful to refrain from comparing experiences of oppression and marginalization or pretending that they are experientially the same. Instead, standing in solidarity with others across markers of human difference is an invitation to see ourselves as multiply located based on various embodiments of human difference, some of which position us as perpetrators and others that position us as targets of oppression.[11]

Our concern in the remainder of this chapter is how microaggressions in ministerial contexts perpetrate the production of evil through the diminishment of human life and how we might strive to constructively address these concerns in our congregations, religious organizations, and institutes of theological education.

Awareness: Recognizing Racial Microaggressions in Ministry

As we said in the last chapter, religious language and symbols provide materials for the creation of the social space that all of us inhabit. When white cultural values and norms become conflated with Christian theological normativity, we may inadvertently communicate insulting, invalidating, and otherwise denigrating messages toward those who identify as racial minorities. Kendall says, "Those of us who are white so frequently fail to remember that everything that happens in our lives occurs in the context of white supremacy—forgetting that reality is one of our most frequently used privileges."[12] We must be attentive to the racial dynamics of our ministerial contexts so that we can begin to overcome the damage of white forgetting and take greater responsibility for the way white supremacy subtly but surely structures our religious spaces and theological imaginations.[13]

Take, for example, Harold's CPE experience. When Harold makes consistent use of black theologians like James Cone and Anthony Pinn, his white peer confronts him with the recommendation that he use more "regular theology" in his papers, going on to name two white theologians he might read and cite. Remember here the dangers of theological hierarchies noted by Farris in the previous chapter. Often our theologies are constructed on a hierarchy of value and worth that serve to reinforce dominant-submissive, privileged-targeted patterns of relationship based on dualistic understandings the world (e.g., male/female, straight/gay, young/old, white/black, wealthy/poor). Recall Farris's statement: "The fundamentally violent dynamic is that we label the other side as ontologically less valuable, therefore more easily disposed of, different, therefore 'other,' and continue hierarchical power based oppressive relationships."[14]

The microaggression Harold receives from his peer is based on this dualistic and hierarchical understanding of value and worth, and it invalidates the legitimacy or sufficiency of theologies that are constructed from the vantage point of black experience. White theologians are considered simply "theologians" or producers of "regular theology," while black theologians are seen as doing something "other," presumably *less than*, "regular theology." The tacit message communicated to Harold is that his theological work is shoddy or incomplete if he is not drawing on the resources of white theologians.

One primary tool of denial in relation to racial microaggressions is the presumption of color blindness. Messages like "I don't see race" are often meant to communicate that one does not see oneself as a racially prejudiced person. These messages have an insidious microaggressive effect. Whenever we are tempted to feign racial color blindness, Sue reminds us that a denial of color is a denial of difference, which is a denial of power and privilege that play on racial differences, which is a denial of personal benefits and advantages that are afforded white persons simply because of their racial group membership.[15] This denial of race is often based on a liberal desire to see human commonality, but it subtly communicates an unwillingness to acknowledge human difference and all of the ways that race structures experience in a cultural milieu shaped by white supremacy. Theologian Fumitaka Matsuoka argues that color blindness toward race "is yet another attempt to appropriate others disguised as a generous act of sensitivity to the plights of racially underrepresented groups."[16]

Harold's white CPE peer couches color blindness in theological language, saying to Harold, "I don't even see you as a black man. I just see you as a human being and a child of God." This microinvalidation, however, communicates the subtle message that Harold's racial experience and all of the ways that race has shaped his life, identity, and theological perspectives are ultimately unimportant and ignorable. Harold's peer presumes that the white theologies he recommends are simply theologically neutral rather than influenced by white racial experience. In actuality, many white theologies simply *ignore* questions of race, which is indicative of the white privilege of "forgetting." As Fernandez explains, "The dominant theology as basically white European American theology is 'color-blind': therefore, it does not factor race into the theological equation." He goes on to argue, however, that "race has to be dealt with because, whether we like it or not, it is a mental grid that colors our theological interpretation."[17]

Assessment: Understanding the Power of Racial Microaggressions to Harm

As we've seen, the dominant white social setting regularly seeks to deny or diminish the importance of race in understanding the daily experiences of life. Kendall reminds us, "If we aren't forced to deal with color—ours or others'—we can pretend that we don't live in a society totally stratified by race."[18] This is true for the wider society, but theological language, symbols, and settings intensify the power of racially based microaggressions to cause harm to our deepest sense of who we are as human beings in relation to other human beings and to an ultimate context.

Matsuoka says, "Particularly for Christians, the question is, How can we honestly confess that we are created as one in the midst of our own racial differences?"[19] He further points us toward a vision of addressing racial differences in such a way that we transcend simple records of discord and rehearsals of victimization, moving toward the cultivation of new resources to constructively address the fragmentation and alienation among racial groups. Ideally, says Matsuoka, this moves us forward in a struggle for the well-being of the whole society.[20] As we strive to move in this way, addressing the fragmentation and alienation perpetuated by racial microaggressions, it is important to assess the potential for harm for both white people and racial minorities.

The Monopoly of Imagination: The Harm to White People

Racism in general and racial microaggressions in particular are harmful not just to racial minorities who are targeted by practices of injustice, oppression, and violence—that is, those who are overtly disadvantaged by the structure of white privilege. As they undergird and legitimate white privilege, they are also harmful to white people—those who are unfairly and even inadvertently advantaged by the status quo. Undoubtedly, the harm performed by unjust social structures and practices of violence are more deleterious to the health and safety of racial minorities, but it is essential that we recognize the way that the well-being of white persons is also diminished by unquestioned white supremacy.

Matsuoka names one aspect of the damage done to white people as a "monopoly of imagination."[21] When white imaginations are shaped so subtly and consistently by white values and norms that are then presumed to be neutral or given rather than shaped by white racial experience, we are induced into overlooking the ways white privilege and supremacy shape our relation to our own sense of self, to others in society, and to our theological imaginations as well. Not only do we suffer in our ability to form communities where difference is respected and valued, but the very minds of white people are formed and deformed by tacit acquiescence to values of white supremacy.

Sue, too, notes the psychological cost to perpetrators. In order to remain in good conscience, perpetrators must engage in a great deal of denial and live within a constructed false reality that ultimately diminishes their ability to understand the experience of marginalized groups.[22] The harm to white perpetrators must also come into view as we address the harm of racial microaggressions in ministerial contexts. Matsuoka argues, "There is . . . an inherent inequality about the foundation of societal coherence. A Christian understanding of peoplehood must proceed with an acknowledgment of this foundational inequality that is woven into the fabric of our society."[23] Only then can we accurately assess the damage done to the lives of others and the harm to our own well-being as white people by racial microaggressions and the racial dynamics they uphold and legitimate.

Kendall notes, "One of the privileges granted to those of us who are white is permission to forget that all of us come into conversations bringing our history and our experiences with us."[24] Thus, we are often unaware of the way our history obscures our ability to see the perpetration of racial microaggressions. Our inability to make assessments with the reality of racial stratification in view often leads to the microinvalidating propensity of white people to minimize microaggressive experiences by explaining them away with nonracial reasons for the incident in question.[25] For example, when Harold expressed concerns about his marginalizing experiences in the hospital and with his peers related to what he believed to be his racial minority status, his CPE supervisor immediately denied that racial dynamics could be at play. Instead, he suggested that Harold's peers and the staff of the hospital were distancing themselves from him because Harold was just coming on a bit too strong.

The Multifaceted Harm to Racial Minorities

The literature on race-based microaggressions is rich with examples of the microaggressions experienced by racial minorities in the United States. For example, there are several commonalities in the microaggressions experienced among Asian, black, and Latino/a people: intellectual stereotyping, treatment as second-class citizens, assumptions of sharing a common experience with other black, Latino/a, Asian people, and a pathologizing of cultural and communication styles.[26] Asian Americans experience microaggressions containing themes of the exotic Asian, of the intelligent Asian, and of being invisible, in contrast to the themes of intellectual inferiority and untrustworthiness often experienced by black targets of microaggressions.[27] Both Asian and Latino/a people regularly experience the microinvalidation of being viewed as an alien in their own land.[28]

The vignette with Victoria contained the microaggressive trope of "alien in their own land." During the service, she was informed about a Spanish language ministry at the church by a well meaning white woman who had made an assumption about Victoria's language preference based on her race. When Victoria admitted that she doesn't speak very good Spanish, the woman then asked how long she had lived in the United States, again assuming that Victoria couldn't have been born here—even though she was.

Microaggressive experiences among racial minorities may lead to the development of a healthy paranoia that makes them attentive to the race-based microaggressions in their immediate environment. In addition, a recipient of microaggressions may perform a sanity check, which involves turning to loved ones or trusted friends and allies in order to gain another perspective on the experience in question—testing their own perception of reality against that of trusted others. This represents an attempt to lessen the attributional ambiguity inherent in microaggressive experience. There is also a tendency to "rescue" offenders, placing their well-being above one's own.[29]

We might imagine that Harold will reach out to African American ministerial colleagues to share his experience of marginalization in the hospital and attempt to discern in dialogue whether his treatment by the clinical team is a microinsult to his pastoral authority as a black minister in a predominantly white setting. Nadal identifies three primary questions a target of microaggressions must typically ask in order to decide what response he or she is willing to make: Did this microaggression really occur?

Should I respond to this microaggression? How should I respond to this microaggression?[30]

We might also imagine that if Harold didn't have the interpersonal resources to perform this sanity check and receive some support in confronting these microaggressive experiences, he might take the advice of his supervisor and rescue his peers from their discomfort with black liberation theological perspectives by drawing on other theological sources and "toning down" his talk about racial dynamics in the hospital setting. If Harold chooses to continue confronting microaggressions when he experiences them, he certainly faces the catch-22 of responding. Nadal describes it this way: "If they do choose to say something, an argument may ensue, which may then lead to psychological discomfort (and potentially even physical safety issues). If they choose not to say something, they may feel regretful and perseverate on their lack of response."[31] Our hope is that helping congregations and communities of faith to openly address the reality of microaggressions may decrease the power of this catch-22 and allow for greater communication about the harm of microaggressions and how their power and prevalence can be diminished.

Action: Cultivating Religious Communities
of Resistance and Resilience

As we proceed into a discussion of engagement, it is helpful to note that we are not proposing strategies for engaging white privilege, racism, and racial justice more broadly. Rather, we are suggesting ways of engaging race-based microaggressions specifically. While the larger social forces of racial oppression, injustice, and violence fund the potential of microaggressive harm, addressing the complexity of these realities in congregations and other institutions is an undertaking that is simply beyond the scope of this book. Learning how we can constructively engage the potential for racial microaggressions in our communities, however, is one important piece of a larger racial justice framework. We can deal with racial justice on a grand scale—addressing mass incarceration, discriminatory institutional and public policies, interpersonal prejudicial attitudes and beliefs, and so forth—but if we fail to attend to racial microaggressions, we have only dealt with the *visibilities* of racism and not the *invisibilities*. To make the invisible visible is a primary goal of microaggressions education.

As Matsuoka suggests, "Central to a Christian understanding of human relationships is the church, which is called and empowered to witness to God's intended wholeness for all creation. The church does this both by transcending in its own life those barriers (e.g., of race and culture) that divide persons from one another and by opposing such barriers in human society."[32] This requires an increased awareness of racial microaggressions in our midst and a careful ability to assess the potential for microaggressions to cause harm within ecclesial contexts. But as Beverly Daniel Tatum reminds us, "Heightening . . . awareness of racism without also developing an awareness of the possibility of change is a prescription for despair. I consider it unethical to do one without the other."[33] Thus, we have two suggestions for cultivating communities with an eye toward the possibility of change.

Communities of Countermemory

Sociologist Patricia Hill Collins tells of teaching a classroom of African American second-graders in the 1970s on the topic of community. The text assigned by the curriculum to teach this lesson was an upbeat book full of pictures of kind white families and plush, green neighborhoods with reassurances of care and safety. Somewhere between this book and her knowledge of her pupils' everyday life experience, Collins became too uncomfortable to continuing reading. She says,

> We all knew that the book and I were lying. So I asked them to tell me about their community as they experienced it. One little boy tentatively raised his hand. To my shock, he shared a story of how, because the housing commission had left the doors open, his best friend had fallen down an elevator chute the day before. His friend had been killed.
>
> At that moment, I faced an important choice. I could teach the status quo, or I could teach for a change. I could not see how I could lie to my students, no matter how pure my intentions. [34]

We face this same choice in all of our congregations and religious institutions: to teach the status quo or to teach for a change.

What Collins did in this vignette is to begin cultivating what Emilie Townes calls "countermemory." Against the grain of the status quo represented in the authorized curriculum for the classroom, she invited her pupils to give witness of a different reality—one that calls for change-oriented action. Townes says, "Countermemory can open up subversive spaces within dominant discourses that expand our sense of who we are and, possibly, create a more whole and just society in defiance of structural evil."[35] As Kendall says to white people, "If we only hear what we are saying, if we only have our perception, we begin to believe that what we're saying is true and that everyone shares our views."[36] Communities of countermemory are characterized by a pluriformity of voices, intentionally circulating in resistance to the stultifying potential of the dominant narratives that induce us into defensive denial of racial microaggressions. Countermemory reminds us that *all* of our experiences are touched by race.

One method of cultivating communities of countermemory is storytelling, like Collins encouraged in her classroom. Matsuoka speaks to its importance: "Storytelling aims at challenging versions of reality put forward by the dominant culture. . . . By putting forward an anecdotal version of reality, that person asserts the primacy of personal experience—and no matter what society tells that person, he or she trusts his or her own personal experiences."[37] We might imagine that if Harold's CPE supervisor were attentive to the cultivation of countermemory within the context of clinical pastoral education, he might encourage the proliferation of theological sources from black, Latino/a, Native American, and Asian theologians, in addition to those from feminist, womanist, and queer scholars. A CPE peer group or other educational space characterized by countermemory will also find ways to increase the ability of participants to bring their own narratival voices into the hearing of others in ways that are honored and respected. While discomfort will arise among group members who are confronted with their own complicity in dynamics of oppression and perpetration of microaggressions, communities where the praxis of countermemory is intentionally cultivated help to curtail the tendency of denial, white "forgetting," and the microinvalidation of racial experience.

Communities of countermemory are not simply beneficial to racial minorities, however. White community members benefit too. As Townes states,

> It is not healthy—not even for the dominant elite—to fail to remember the textures of our common humanity. To ignore, as it were, the vast and varied terrains that comprise not only the strands of our histories but also the concrete materialities of our existence throttles our humanity in creation. It is strategic in that to "forget" is to be able to feign ignorance and lack of agency.[38]

This systemic forgetting that is a component of white privilege is a prime dynamic fueling the deniability so prevalent when white persons are confronted with microaggressions. Countermemory provides a source of resistance to this forgetting, says Townes, as it "insists that to deconstruct and eradicate systems of evil demands that we engage in exposing the truth of the multiplicities that form us—nationally and globally—with as much precision as we can."[39]

Of course, cultivating communities of countermemory can prove difficult. This is especially true for predominantly white faith communities whose collective imagination has been profoundly shaped by Matsuoka's "monopoly of imagination." Here again, Townes encourages us to face these challenges by exploring the concrete experiences of others openly and empathically:

> Though it presents profound challenges to our ability to see and analyze, experience deals with concrete material existence, not abstractions. This challenges us to move beyond ourselves to develop empathy *and* respect for others and, more importantly, for the creation of public policy, to *share* in the experience of others. . . . In short, we need each other to help us understand the worlds we have created and are creating. . . . This invitation to growth, as it were, admits that we are a complex of historical interactions on a cosmic playing field.[40]

For predominantly white classrooms, churches, and other religious communities, including the voices of Asian, black, indigenous, or Latino/a people within lessons, sermons, or liturgies is not simply a matter of *aesthetics*— making more "colorful" an otherwise whitewashed presentation of reality. The intentional inclusion of perspectives from racial difference is a matter of *ethics*—expanding the circle of persons giving testimony to the reality of the world in which we all live. If these racially diverse elements serve only to adorn our services with "exotic" beauty and never penetrate our epistemology, we are performing a microaggression of exoticization that has a long history within white communities.

For white members of communities that privilege countermemory, the effect is overcoming the false consciousness inculcated by white privilege and breaking the monopoly on white imagination by the introduction of many and varied stories, narratives, theologies, and lived experiences from other racial vantage points. This moves us toward experiences of discomfort and distress over our unearned advantage that, consequently, diminishes the lives of others and provokes us toward acts of solidarity in dismantling racial structures of injustice.

Communities of Solidarity, Lamentation, and Healing

As we assess our own religious institutions and communities for the potential of microaggressive violence, we must remember that members of our faith communities and religious institutions are also members of a wider social sphere in which they live their daily lives amid a great deal of microaggressive communication. Our communities of faith hold great potential to become places of resistance and healing in addressing these common, everyday experiences of microaggressive violence.[41]

Healing from the harm of racial microaggressions cannot take place in communities where the practice of denial is a protected privilege of the white majority. Matsuoka says, "Our challenge is not merely a struggle against an unjust society that stifles dignity. The challenge is to move out of silence and recover speech, which permits communion with one another—breaking bread together, for which people so deeply yearn and which we Christians confess to be our deeply held value."[42] Moving out of silence and recovering speech is a practice of *making the invisible visible* in our communities of faith.

One oft forgotten theological practice that serves to make the invisibilities of suffering visible to a community of faith is *lamentation*, the raising of voices in outrage over social evil that characterizes what Matsuoka calls "a hope against hope born out of bewailing."[43] Microaggressions' inherent attributional ambiguity and easy deniability threaten to silence the voices of those harmed by their subtle violence. A communally created space for bringing these experiential realities into speech actively resists the insidious silencing that keeps microaggressions out of sight and out of mind for the dominant majority.

But bringing these experiences to expression for those targeted is a risky practice (remember the catch-22 of responding). Voicing microaggressive experiences risks bringing criticism, denial, and further microaggressive invalidation if others in the community are not willing to hear the voices of hurt, anger, and lamentation. Thus, cultivating this space for lamentation of microaggressive violence requires an *ethic of solidarity*. As M. Shawn Copeland says, "Through a praxis of solidarity, we not only apprehend and are moved by the suffering of the other, we confront and address its oppressive cause and shoulder the other's suffering. . . . Solidarity sets the dynamics of love against the dynamics of domination."[44]

Solidarity is a robust theological response to suffering that is forged by intentional and very difficult work within community. That is why we said in chapter 1 that addressing microaggressions in faith communities cannot be reduced to an act of "political correctness." Indeed, political correctness is an anemic vision for any congregation or religious community responding to a sense of call toward a purposeful cultivation of a community in which "a hope against hope born out of bewailing" can be brought to voice. But solidarity in suffering can't be practiced in silence. Shouldering the other's suffering in solidarity and making the invisibilities of suffering visible through lamentation is a robust, justice-oriented response to the violence of microaggressive communication. Part of this "shouldering" responsibility for white community members is accepting that feelings of guilt, shame, and anger will, at times, arise.[45] But we must work through these responses in community without allowing them to coax us back into practices of enforced silencing and denial.

In addition to the healing potential this holds for individual community members, it also works toward the strengthening of our communities themselves. Kendall argues that institutions and organizations that cultivate the capability to keep topics of race and white privilege as part of larger conversations develop an enhanced ability to interpret situations and make decisions as an organization. She further argues for the benefits of this institutional ability: "Additionally, the organization would gain a higher degree of honesty in conversations, meetings, and feedback as well as more respect for speaking the truth, even if it means making others uncomfortable."[46]

We hope that this brief treatment of the importance of countermemory and communities of solidarity, lamentation, and healing will not make cultivating this type of community seem a simple and easily achievable task. Indeed, it is difficult work! It is also work that cannot be undertaken alone but must be situated within a community of others who shoulder the burden with one another and support one another on the journey. But despite the hard work that is required to cultivate such communities, we hope that it seems possible and well worth the risk entailed in making the invisibilities of racial microaggressions visible in our communities of faith and religious institutions.

Chapter 4

Microaggressions and Gender

Ministerial Microaggressions in Action

Gendered Roles, Overlooked Talents

*M*aci, a woman in her late forties, recently joined a new church. She couldn't wait to become more involved in the church's various ministries. As a bank president, she assumed she'd have much to offer to the finance and stewardship committee. And though high school was many years ago, she had fond memories of performing in theater and public speaking classes, so she was also interested in serving as a lay liturgist, reading Scripture in worship, or otherwise having a vocal and active role on Sunday mornings. When she sat down with her new deacon to discuss her potential involvement in church, he began by saying, "We could really use more Sunday school teachers in the children's department. And I'm sure you'll be interested in serving on the hospitality committee; they make all the food for Wednesday night supper."

Maci actually eats out almost every day because she deplores cooking and, though she has two children at home, she has no interest in or training for teaching children's classes. Her deacon never asked what she does for a living or what ministries excited her most. She questioned whether she should have joined the church if her deacon expressed no interest in getting to know her, ignored her skills and gifts, and expected her to fulfill traditional gender roles assigned to women. Though her deacon is supposed to be the leader she goes to for pastoral care or church-related concerns, she felt that bringing up her issues would create a wedge between them or that he wouldn't understand.

Invisible Training

Andrea has been a clergywoman for twenty years. She serves as a senior pastor, has a PhD in religion, and teaches a course at a local seminary. Andrea was asked to serve as a panelist with two other clergy and a social worker in her community to discuss homelessness. The moderator introduced each person before the panel began. He referred to both of her male colleagues as "Rev." and the social worker as "Mr." When introducing Andrea, he simply called her "Andrea." Throughout the panel discussion, Andrea was routinely referred to by her first name, while her male colleagues were addressed by their titles followed by their last name.

Andrea felt invalidated and overlooked, as though her ordination and education were not as important as those of her male colleagues. Though she has worked in ministry for as long as her male colleagues and actually has more education, her titles were left off the printed program and oral introduction. She wanted to speak up on behalf of all women who are overlooked, but she feared she might sound snobby for highlighting her own credentials. Since humility is such an important virtue in Christian ministry, she opted not to say anything, though she feared that other women at the event may have noticed and felt disempowered by her silence.

Clergywomen Speak Up

Upon asking a professional group of clergywomen about their experiences with microaggressions in ministry, we received nearly one hundred responses describing interactions that range from well intentioned to passive-aggressive, stereotypical to painful. Whether they have to do with appearance, ability, or motherhood, clergywomen experience microaggressions on a regular basis.

"How will you be a good mom and a pastor?" one senior pastor was asked after the birth of her first child. Her husband is also a pastor, but no one seemed concerned about the balance of his pastoral and parenting duties.

"Now that you're engaged, are you planning to get pregnant?" a search committee asked another young clergywoman during an interview.

"We've got the prettiest minister around. That will help us bring new members because everyone will enjoy looking at her in the pulpit," a church member said.

"What's under that sexy black dress?" a church member asked his pastor while pointing at her black clerical robe.

When a pastor expressed concern to the sound crew that her microphone wasn't working properly, a man at the soundboard said to another crew member, "She's so pretty, it doesn't really matter what she says."

"Women shouldn't shovel snow," the senior pastor told his female associate one February morning in Minnesota.

"Don't move the tables and chairs before Wednesday night supper," a member told her athletic female pastor. "It's not ladylike."

"Are you sure you want to schedule your sermon so far in advance?" a male senior pastor asked his female associate. "What if you're having your period that day?"

Male Privilege

As these vignettes and examples from clergywomen illustrate, sexism is not a thing of the past. Rather, women encounter modern sexism on a regular basis. Before delving into the details of modern sexism and microaggressions addressed at women, it is imperative to offer a brief glimpse at the notion of male privilege.

Male privilege refers to the unearned political, social, and economic advantages granted to men based solely on their gender. These same advantages are routinely denied to women. As indicated in the previous chapter on racial microaggressions, a man's access to these benefits also depends on his race, ethnicity, sexual orientation, and ability. Often what makes male privilege so problematic is that most men are unaware of their own privilege and even deny its existence, claiming instead that men are actually the ones who are disadvantaged in society. Many think of sexism as an individual act of exclusion or meanness, and while this can be true, male privilege is part of a wider invisible system that affords power and dominance to men at the expense of women.

Sexism and patriarchy are not only about a system whereby women experience interpersonal prejudice, systemic injustice, and violence based on their gender. Sexism and patriarchy are also part of a system of advantage for men in a society structured by a legacy of gendered injustice that privileges white men over everyone else. What is more, maleness is understood and accepted as normative. The dominant cultural message portrays maleness as neutral, whereas being female is derivative of being male.[1] This is evident in our language and, in the case of ministry, embedded in much of our foundational theology. For example, many churches bolster their claims that women should not hold ministerial leadership positions—or any position outside of the home—by claiming that Eve was a derivative of Adam, having been formed from his rib. Adam (man) has the neutral privilege, while Eve (woman) is a lesser version; a binary is created, and a subsequent hierarchy ensues. Male is privileged at the expense of female. The male as the benchmark for normalcy is also embedded in much of the history of Christian theology. For example, Thomas Aquinas believed that the female body was a deficient or "failed" male body.[2]

Evidence of male privilege is found throughout society. Whether it is the fact that women still earn three-quarters less than men, hold only 10 percent of elected offices in the United States, or hold only 15 percent of Fortune 500 board seats, it is clear that men are afforded more societal privileges.[3] What is more, a so-called stained-glass ceiling exists for women in ministry. This explains why, though about half of all Protestant traditions are willing to ordain women, only 15.5 percent of clergy in the United States are women.[4] Whether it is all-male leadership, disproportionately higher male compensation, antiwoman theology, or male-exclusive language, male privilege continues to reign supreme within the hallowed walls of the institutions that claim to nurture our faith. This privileging is the foundation on which much of gendered microaggressions rest. Without shattering this phallocentric foundation, addressing the complexities of microaggressions will be virtually impossible.

Awareness: Recognizing Gendered Microaggressions in Ministry

Since women are afforded more opportunities than ever—the rights to vote, work outside the home, play sports, attend universities, and even become ordained in some faith traditions—many assume that sexism is history. It is considered bigoted, small-minded, and backward to say and do overtly sexist things in our society. Old-fashioned sexism, or believing and treating women as inferior and with smaller brains, for example, has given way to modern sexism. Although modern sexism is not as overt and intentional as old-fashioned sexism, these subtler and microaggressive forms of sexism exert power over women, contributing negatively to their social, psychological, economic, political, and spiritual well-being.

As Derald Wing Sue describes it, modern sexism is a "denial of personal bias and prejudice toward women, a general conscious belief in equality of the sexes, but unconscious attitudes that foster nonsupport for programs and legislation helpful to women."[5] A specific form of modern sexism is benevolent sexism. Benevolent sexists are "motivated paternalistically to 'protect the weaker sex,' view them as objects of 'romantic love,' and admire them as 'wives and mothers.' Despite viewing women positively, it is based on an idealized stereotyped perception of the opposite sex and is equally harmful."[6] Take, for example, the senior pastor who told his female associate that women should not shovel snow, or the congregant who told her athletic female pastor that moving tables "isn't ladylike." Though both clergywomen were certainly capable and willing to do these physical tasks, benevolent sexism was so embedded that the pastor and member felt that the women should avoid physical labor in favor of "ladylike" decorum or propriety.

Gender microaggressions are forms of modern sexism. These microaggressions are subtle and sometimes even unnoticed by both perpetrator and target. It is precisely their invisibility and ambiguity that make them so difficult to navigate. Sue identifies nine themes with regard to gender microaggressions.[7] Based on qualitative research, we will add a tenth theme stemming primarily from ministry settings.

1. Sexual objectification. Sexual objectification is perceiving the female body as an object for pleasure or reducing a woman's entire being to her physical appearance or sexuality. In secular settings, this is demonstrated in catcalling or staring at a woman's breasts or backside. No matter their age, race, sexuality, or attire, virtually all women experience such objectification at some point in their lives, and many experience such behavior on a regular basis. One would hope that this behavior would never occur within the confines of a church, denominational body, or seminary. As some of the opening examples noted, such is clearly not the case. While the example of asking the pastor what she's wearing under her sexy black dress (that is, her clerical robe) may seem a bit extreme, countless women experience objectification by fellow Christians. It might be easy to dismiss concerns over such incidents as being overly sensitive. "Clearly the person who made those comments was just giving you a compliment about your appearance; you should be flattered instead of offended," some may say. Though it is true that most folks truly intend statements directed at a woman's appearance as compliments, it is important to remember the way women are routinely objectified sexually by the wider society. With this in mind, one may see why a woman could feel offended or objectified when someone made comments about her hair, weight, or outfit after she led or participated in worship. Such a compliment, while intended to be flattering, could make her feel as though her appearance is more important than what she has to say.

2. Second-class citizenship. Gender microaggressions in this category involve verbal, behavioral, and environmental communications that do not give women the same opportunities as men. This category may well be the most prevalent in ministry. Many denominations do not permit women to become ordained or to hold particular leadership positions, thus treating them as less than men. Though some denominations celebrate women's ordination and opportunities for leadership, clergywomen still experience lower pay, less access to resources, and smaller networks of support and mentorship than men within the same denomination. Similarly, if all the positions of power in an institution—whether it is pastor in a church, dean of a seminary, or president of a denomination—are held by men, women still experience second-class citizenship even if those positions are technically open to them.

3. Use of sexist language. Sue highlights the way *man* is used as a neutral referent in everyday life in terms such as *chairman, policeman,* or *mailman.* Similarly, *man* or *mankind* is often used when referencing humanity. Sexist language of this manner continues to occur routinely, even though guides to proper English style repudiated it long ago. Interestingly, women who hold positions of power typically associated with men, such as doctors, pilots, or attorneys, are often referred to as "lady doctors," "women pilots," or "female attorneys," as though their gender makes them less worthy of their occupational title than men.

We contend that the use of sexist language is close in line behind second-class citizenship in the way women experience microaggressions in ministry settings. The role of inclusive language continues to be a hot-button issue in many churches, seminaries, and denominations. It is such a seemingly contentious issue that it is worth deeper consideration here.

Inclusive language is defined in opposition to exclusive language. According to Sharon Warner, exclusive language is "language which holds up one particular entity or reality as the norm for all other entities or realities; it functions to establish one particular as universal and generic." Inclusive language, by contrast, is "language which permits particulars."[8] When a preacher uses inclusive language, she recognizes the history of oppression embodied in gendered language for humanity and God. Accordingly, she uses her words to subvert and overturn such domination.

Warner notes that inclusive language falls into two categories. The first is inclusive language that is neutral. The second is that which is particular. Most churches, denominational bodies, or seminaries that promote the use of inclusive language choose the first option. In these cases, preachers and liturgists use gender-neutral terms such as *human, humankind, person,* and *people.* Similarly, God is referred to as *God* rather than the commonly used *he* or *him.* Warner contends, however, that neutrality is not enough. She nuances her argument with regard to particular inclusive language for God:

> Particular inclusive language for reference to God needs further exploration here. *Please,* hear me clearly. The philosophy of inclusive language does critique the use of the particularity of Father language for God as exclusive. However, the critique of Father language for God is *not* that it is

exclusive by virtue of its being particular, but that it is exclusive by virtue of its claim to being universal. Father language for God functions oppressively for many people by virtue of its claim to serve as the normative particular which all should have. Thus, the problem with Father language for God is *not* that it expresses a particular view of God. That is its power and that is what must be claimed. But, its particularity must be exposed. For too long its particularity has been *masked* as it has been promoted as a universal and generic view of God. When particularity is masked it is never problematized. We never see that there might be a problem with this particular (or any particular) functioning as a name for God. As many have noted, our failure to problematize a particular leads to idolatry, to equation of that particular with God. To expose the particularity of Father language for God we need to place it alongside many other particular names and images, for only alongside many other particulars can it be seen as *only* one other particular and, therefore, as participative in the human problem of calling God by any name.[9]

Karen Stroup bolsters Warner's claim by emphasizing what most congregants actually hear or think of when neutralized inclusive language is employed in liturgy. Stroup suggests that when we carefully replace *he* and *his* with *God* and *God's*, most people still hear with their internal perceptive ear *he* and *his*, because referencing God in this way has been normalized and universalized for centuries.[10] Marjorie Procter-Smith agrees: "Gender-neutral referents tend to be heard as male unless they are stereotypically female. The use of *God* as if it were gender-neutral does not challenge the prevailing belief that God is male."[11] In these ways, neutral inclusive language continues to allow socialized patterns of domination to shape perceptions of God and humanity. If men and women were truly treated equally, and if an equal number of people perceived God to be female as male, then such neutral language could work. But women and men are not treated equally in society, and certainly not in the church, and most people still perceive God in male terms. Until this shifts, neutral language can actually contribute to gender microaggressions within the church.

We have shared such perspectives with people in many congregations, proclaiming them from the pulpit in a way that was liberating for many. In some cases, however, someone inevitably brings up charges of a double standard, claiming that such particular language risks reverse sexism or that it excludes the voice of men. We turn again to the thoughtful nuance of Warner's argument for particularity.

First, she explains that claiming a particularity is not oppressive. So calling God *Mother* is not oppressive to men. But to claim that a particularity is universal is to oppress. So calling God *Mother* at the expense of *Father* in a world where *Mother* is the common understanding of God would be oppressive to men. But we do not reside in such a world. "Indeed," says Warner, "anyone religiously formed in this era experiences the Mother image as a particular, not as a universal. Reverse oppression, or any oppression, is not what is happening here."[12] Second, noting that the historic male language for humanity and God has functioned oppressively in ways that keep women from flourishing, prevent women from ordination, and sustain all-male power structures, Warner concludes, "The probability in the use of feminine language for God for a similar oppression of men is dubious given the continual male dominated social and religious life in which we reside. In this present historic context, the preferential cultivation of what has been silenced, specifically feminine images of God, functions to balance not to oppressively exclude."[13]

Though the use of inclusive language continues to be a source of debate even among those in liberal denominations, it is worth noting that Sue calls this a form of microaggression "sexist language." It is not biblical language. It is not theological language. It is sexist language, and it has no place in ministry.

4. Assumption of inferiority. Within the confines of modern or benevolent sexism, women are valued for interpersonal skills, nurturing, and caring, but they are often considered inferior intellectually, temperamentally, and physically. In the case of Maci, who just joined a new church, it is unlikely that her male deacon would explicitly say that he believed women are bad at math but skilled at teaching children. However, based solely on her gender, he assumed that Maci would be good at working with children or in the kitchen rather than serving on the finance committee. While some may say that such an inference is too great a leap, it is important to remember what women like Maci are told regularly by society: that women are not good at math, women are better caregivers for children, and women are better suited for working in the kitchen. In a culture that sends out such messages from media, commercials, and teachers on a daily basis, it is not difficult to imagine that Maci's deacon may have absorbed them.

The assumption of inferiority is also a factor in the senior pastor's questioning of his associate about why she is planning her preaching so far in advance when she may be menstruating at that time. Not only is such a comment wildly inappropriate, but it also assumes that this educated, capable, trained woman will be unable to preach effectively because her temperament will be hampered by her period. Similar claims have been launched by pundits who think that a woman could not be a capable president, so it is no surprise that people in the church behave similarly.

5. Restrictive gender roles. Restrictive gender microaggressions are similar to assumptions of inferiority in that they are based on the belief that women should be soft, feminine, caring, and domestic. Breaking such gender roles can have negative consequences. A man who is assertive in a meeting is viewed as having a "take charge" personality, as competent, and as an excellent leader. A woman who exhibits those same behaviors is seen as "bitchy," "unladylike," or "overly emotional." A microaggression that adheres to restrictive gender roles is evident in the example of the senior pastor who expressed her opinion on a church matter and then was told that she was bossy and that assertiveness is a good attribute for men but not for women. As the pastor of the church, she felt that holding firm opinions regarding the church's well-being should be an expected leadership quality, but those holding to restrictive gender roles wanted her to sit quietly and not voice her opinions.

6. Denial of the reality of sexism. The denial of the reality of sexism is a primary example of a microinvalidation. Women's experiences of sexism are viewed as wrong and invalid. Sue notes that this denial is sent to women in five ways: "(1) sexism is a thing of the past, (2) women are actually 'advantaged' in our society, (3) those who complain about sexism are oversensitive, (4) women are externalizing their own shortcomings or unhappiness, and (5) perpetrators trivialize sexist incidents."[14] This type of microaggression is most prevalent in progressive denominations and churches that boldly and firmly ordain women yet are often unwilling to acknowledge the ways women are still underrepresented or mistreated within their organization. For example, a young woman in seminary is awarded a full scholarship; she has a 4.0 GPA, she wrote excellent application essays, she has stellar recommendation letters, and she even has some experience working in a local church. She is approached by a group of her male peers during her first week of seminary and told that the only reason she received the full scholarship rather than one of her male peers is because she is a woman. These students attend a seminary that prides itself on its inclusion of women in ministry. Yet the male students in this example deny the reality of sexism and instead claim that women are afforded special privileges.

7. Denial of individual sexism. The denial of individual sexism can occur through deliberate denial or while sincerely believing that one is not behaving in a sexist manner. One who deliberately denies one's own sexism may hold hostile or negative views of women but cover these views to appear less sexist. An example could be a man claiming that a male job applicant appears more qualified than a female even when the two candidates have the same credentials. Sue asserts that the majority of microaggressions that deny individual sexism are from men "who sincerely believe they are not sexist, profess equality for women, and consciously abhor sex discrimination."[15] Because of male privilege, it can be very difficult for some men to acknowledge when they have behaved in a sexist manner because they don't want to appear bigoted or close-minded. Recognizing that we are all influenced by our wider sexist society is a first step in acknowledging that even the most thoughtful men still have the capacity to say and do sexist things.

8. Invisibility. Women in corporate America have often described feeling invisible in the workplace. In this circumstance, women feel unimportant, powerless, and overlooked. Inasmuch as invisibility is a problem for women in wider society, it is doubled in ministry settings. In quite a few denominations, women experience invisibility because there are absolutely no women in leadership positions. Women are literally invisible when it comes to hiring candidates, searching for leaders, or pooling volunteers. When women are not even permitted to lead, volunteer for positions that have authority over men, or become ordained, they do not simply experience invisibility; they are blatantly made invisible by the institution. Even within progressive faith communities that stand for equality, women may still feel overlooked, powerless, or unimportant because they see far more men than women in positions of power and authority. Take Andrea, for example, the clergywoman who had been ordained for twenty years and held a PhD in religion. When she was serving on a panel with her male colleagues and was referred to routinely by her first name even though the male panelists were consistently addressed as "Rev." or "Mr.," Andrea felt as though her being, training, education, and ordination were invisible. Though she sat on the same panel and held the same qualifications as her male peers, her presence was minimized.

9. Sexist humor. Sue opens his section on sexist humor by referring to a common joke made by a male superior when a female employee asks "How can I help?" in reference to a work project. The male boss replies by saying, "Just stand there and look pretty." This attempt at humor is similar to when the member of the sound crew said that whether the pastor's microphone worked was not an issue because everyone just wanted to look at how pretty she was. Similarly, one can assume that the comment from a member who asked his pastor what she was wearing under her "sexy black dress" was intended as a joke, but it clearly was not funny or appropriate. Sexist jokes are not harmless or humorous; instead, they demean women and perpetuate unfair stereotypes.

10. Antiwoman theology and biblical interpretation. In addition to the nine types of gender microaggressions articulated by Derald Wing Sue, we would like to add a tenth that applies to ministry settings: antiwoman theology and biblical interpretation. As we articulated in chapter 2, microaggressions take on theological weight that assaults the soul when they are perpetuated in ministerial settings. Unfortunately, church is one of the few places where we are willing to tolerate intolerance in the name of tolerating everyone's perspective. There are many Christians who uphold liberated social roles for women—working outside the home, holding prestigious leadership positions in business and politics, and so forth—but whose theology maintains that women should not hold positions of leadership within the church. Most who adhere to such an antiwoman theology assert that this worldview stems from a literal interpretation of the Bible. Traditionalists who maintain such a theological and biblical perspective claim that God made women and men differently and that men's roles entail ministerial leadership but that women's roles do not. Through the lens of microaggressions, such a theology is clearly gender-biased and sexist. This theology and the interpretation of Scripture that undergirds it are oppressive, invalidating, and hurtful to women. An individual, church, denomination, or seminary that tolerates such harmful theology and biblical interpretation is guilty of microaggression against women. It is not simply the individual or institution that professes such beliefs that is hurting women, but individuals and institutions—even if they do not affirm such a theology—that allow for such exclusive theology are also doing a disservice to women.

Assessment: Understanding the Power of Gender Microaggressions to Harm

Now that we are aware of the different types of gender microaggressions, it is important to assess their power to do harm. What are the impacts of gender microaggressions within ministerial settings? Microaggressions are difficult to address precisely because of their subtlety and ambiguity. Kevin Nadal describes the three primary questions a target of microaggressions must typically ask in order to address such ambiguity: "Did this microaggression really occur?" "Should I respond to this microaggression?" "How should I respond to this microaggression?"[16] Within this line of questioning, a woman may wonder, Did I hear that person correctly? Surely he didn't mean it the way it sounded to me. Am I being too sensitive? I know he is a feminist, so he must not have intended to be so hurtful. The continuous asking of these questions is part of what makes microaggressions so harmful. The victim is constantly expending emotional, psychological—and in ministerial settings, spiritual—energy examining and reexamining her experiences of invalidations and insults. Such constant psychological energy can take a mental, physical, and emotional toll on women (and all victims of microaggressive behavior).

As with racial minorities, microaggressive experiences among women may lead to the development of a healthy paranoia, making one attentive to the gender-based microaggressions in the immediate environment. Some women may approach each church they visit with such paranoia. "So many churches have excluded me that I must prepare myself for exclusion here too," a woman may think when walking into a sanctuary for worship at a new church for the first time. In addition, the recipient of microaggressions may perform a sanity check, which involves turning to loved ones or trusted friends and allies in order to gain another perspective on the experience in question. Such sanity checks were evident when we polled a group of clergywomen for their experiences with gender microaggressions. In an open forum, many shared some of the experiences that began this chapter and then would add comments such as, "Am I crazy or did this really happen?" "Did he actually say that, or did I imagine it?" "Does this man seriously think it's okay for an ordained minister to talk like that?" "Am I overreacting?"

Psychologists have long known that sexism has detrimental effects on women's lives. Sue asserts that sexism negatively impacts women's standard of life, physical health, psychological health, depression, anxiety, stress, and body image, and that it even exacerbates eating disorders.[17] What is more, scholars who study microaggressions claim that overt sexists are actually not the ones who are the most harmful to women. The reason is that women often know how to protect themselves in the face of overt sexism. "This guy is a sexist pig. Who cares what he says?" a woman may think, confident that the man's bigoted attitude is not held by the majority of her friends, colleagues, or even society in general. Instead, it is gender microaggressions that prove the most detrimental to physical, emotion, psychological, and spiritual health. When a woman believes that she is affirmed and loved, she feels safe in the person, community, or institution's presence. She believes that she is valued. When that person, community, or institution acts contrary to what it claims — in the form of gender microaggressions — the woman must address all those questions Nadal posed. Maci, for example, believed that she was joining a church that affirmed and validated women. She believed this so fully that she approached the meeting with her new deacon with enthusiasm, eager to share her ideas for becoming involved in the church's ministries. She felt invalidated upon learning that the church she thought affirmed her instead behaved in a manner that was the opposite.

Women like Maci, who assume they are part of a faith community that values women, find it doubly difficult to navigate gender microaggressions.

When these microaggressions continue to occur, women experience detrimental physical, psychological, and spiritual health issues. Microaggressive stress and physiological stress correlate. Coronary heart disease, hypertension, headaches, weight gain, and sleeplessness can be attributed to dealing with the stress of gender microaggressions at the physical level.[18] On the psychological level, twice as many women as men suffer from depression, and with the exception of obsessive-compulsive disorder, more women suffer from anxiety disorders than men.[19] Additionally, the role of sexual objectification contributes to a host of psychological issues related to body image and eating disorders for women. When these physical and psychological concerns are layered on top of spiritual health, women experience a host of harm from the very institutions and communities that are supposed to nurture and support them.

In the face of possible hypertension, sleeplessness, depression, anxiety, and spiritual drain, the resounding answer to the sanity-check question posed by one clergywoman—"Am I overreacting?"—is "No!" A woman is not overreacting when she refuses to tolerate sexist jokes. A woman is not overreacting when she says she feels invisible within a faith community that lacks women in leadership. A woman is not overreacting when she is irritated by a male colleague who claims that sexism is history. Gender microaggressions have the potential to do physical, psychological, and spiritual harm. Such harm warrants a big reaction. But how should churches, denominations, and seminaries react?

Action: Cultivating Communities of Resistance and Resilience

The damage from gender microaggressions is great. Such damage demands change. Drawing from Derald Wing Sue's three-pronged approach to overcoming gender microaggressions, we propose a four-pronged approach for individuals and for churches, denominations, and seminaries who wish to become communities of resistance and resilience that value women fully. This approach is individual, organizational, theological, and societal.

If you are reading this book, you have taken a first step in acknowledging gender microaggressions. In order to overcome gender microaggressions and engage communities in acts of resistance, we must first become aware of our own stereotypes, biases, and prejudices about women and their roles in ministry and society. Culture impacts us all, and sexist attitudes about women become socialized in us at a young age. To address this cultural conditioning, one must honestly examine beliefs, values, and attitudes toward women and gender roles. Challenge yourself. Be open to change. Question the ways you interact with women. Raise children outside of traditional gender binaries, acknowledging the multiplicity of roles people can play in the world no matter their gender. Break traditional gender roles. Listen to the experiences of women. As you listen, remember that women's experiences are not monolithic. If a woman tells you your actions have been hurtful or sexist, listen to the reasons why rather than quickly trying to defend your position.

The second prong involves organizations. In our case, such an organization is likely a church, seminary, or denominational group. In order to address and overcome gender microaggressions, organizations first must have a policy, a vision, or a mission statement that clearly affirms their nondiscrimination policies with regard to gender. Leadership must be inclusive of women, and organizations should have a proactive role in recruiting and retaining women in leadership positions. They must also provide education and training that includes ways of dealing with sexism in ministry; include other policies, such as parental leave and access to psychological health benefits, that acknowledge the complexity of women's experiences; and develop an inclusive language policy that does not tolerate sexist language at an individual or organizational level.

The third prong deviates from traditional microaggressions literature and is directed only at ministerial settings. In addition to a personal and organizational approach, a theological approach is necessary in properly addressing gender microaggressions in church-related settings. Such an approach directly relates to the antiwoman theology addressed in the first section of this chapter. Organizational policies alone will do little work if they do not stem from and reinforce a theology that affirms and values women. This third prong requires a number of steps: Utilize the work of feminist theological and biblical scholars and highlight this work alongside that of male theologians and biblical scholars rather than in a derivative or reactionary form. Make sure that feminist, womanist, and mujerista theology permeates your preaching, worship planning, pedagogy, curriculum, leadership structure, spiritual formation, and so forth. In so doing, develop what many feminist biblical scholars have referred to as a hermeneutic of suspicion. Question why the Bible says what it says about women. Learn about the sociohistorical contexts present throughout Scripture. The admonition of feminist Bible scholar April DeConick rings true for organizations seeking to create a theology that values women: "As long as the Bible's devaluation of the female body as part of the natural order of creation is viewed as sacred, as holy misogyny, no reasonable argument can dislodge it. . . . How much longer must women suffer the dreadful and damning consequences of the ancient male imagination, which valorized the male body while it vulgarized the female, because the Bible tells us so?"[20] Develop theologies and approaches to Scripture that value women and their experiences of faith rather than harming and invalidating them.

After addressing gender microaggressions on a personal, organizational, and theological level, we are prepared for the fourth prong: the societal. This could also be called the political, particularly since feminists have long proclaimed that the personal is political. Individuals and organizations that seek to rage against the harms of gender microaggressions must also work for drastic societal change. Social policies and legislation must be passed to give women equal opportunities. Political, educational, and corporate systems must shift in ways that honor and value women. React in such a way that these changes can occur. Galvanize your community, your church, and your denomination to work for these changes. Write your state and local representatives. Vote for candidates who value women's rights. Volunteer with organizations that empower women.

We are confident that when enough of us address gender microaggressions personally, organizationally, theologically, and socially, change will come. Perhaps then we will create a world that embodies Galatians 3:28, where there is no longer Jew and Gentile, slave and free, male and female, for all are one in Christ Jesus.

Chapter 5

Microaggressions and Sexual Orientation and Gender Identity

Ministerial Microaggressions in Action

Transition, Family, and Loss

*D*ave, a female-to-male transgender man, is no longer in contact with his biological parents or siblings because when he came out as transgender, they reacted very negatively. His father became physically violent with him. His mother disowned him. And his younger brother, who is a gay cisgender man, told him that he was destroying his body by transitioning. Dave always thought that he would never find a new form of family because he believed that all churches disapproved of his gender identity. Dave became overjoyed when he attended a local Pride celebration and saw a booth sponsored by a church. At first he was skeptical, assuming the church representatives were in attendance to convert all the LGBTQ sinners. As he inched closer to the booth, he noticed members wearing rainbow stickers and a pastor waving a rainbow flag. Dave couldn't believe this was possible!

After talking with the people at the booth, Dave decided to visit the church. He was moved to tears in worship as he looked around and saw families with parents of the same gender worshiping together. He learned that the church had some special ministries specifically for LGBTQ people, such as a support group. He attended and, though he was the only transgender person present, he felt good knowing that the possibility of building a new kind of family existed. For the next year, Dave poured his heart into the congregation. He read Scripture aloud in worship, volunteered on service projects, attended Sunday school, and even once shared his testimony in worship. In sharing his testimony, he outed himself as transgender. After doing so, he received applause, hugs of support, and handshakes of affirmation. During his first Thanksgiving as a member of the church, he was invited by his new friends to share the holiday meal together. As he gathered around the table, Dave knew he had found his new family.

It was no surprise that Dave accepted the nomination to become a deacon one year later. When the time came for a congregational vote on the new board of deacons, Dave won by a landslide. He was thrilled and couldn't wait to begin his new leadership role at the church he now considered family. As Dave shifted into his leadership position, however, he began to notice things he hadn't previously, and he started to feel uncomfortable. A fellow member who attended the LGBTQ support group began to nag Dave incessantly, asking what his "real name" was. This person was referring to the name given to Dave at birth, a name typically assigned to a girl. Dave knew there was nothing constructive the member could do with his birth name and wanted very much to move past that part of his life and live fully into his authentic self: Dave, a man. Another member kept insisting that Dave and his female partner were in a "lesbian relationship" because Dave was "biologically female." Dave felt invalidated, as though the person clearly didn't acknowledge the difference between being lesbian (a sexual orientation) and being trans (a gender identity).

Comments such as these continued to occur, and Dave felt increasingly uneasy. He thought he was at an affirming church, so why did he feel so unaffirmed? He began to make excuses for why he couldn't attend Sunday school, because he no longer felt safe with people in the class who asked him these questions. His anxiety increased so dramatically that he began taking medication. But he continued serving as a deacon and attending worship, insistent that his new family loved and accepted him. One day, Dave asked the deacons to keep him in their prayers, as he was undergoing medical treatment in the upcoming week. After the deacons' meeting, one of the pastors approached Dave regarding his upcoming treatment. The pastor assumed that Dave was referencing gender reassignment surgery. Rather than allowing Dave to explain that he was simply nervous about a routine dental procedure, the pastor blatantly asked Dave about the appearance of his genitals, asking repeatedly for details regarding his transition surgery. Dave felt violated, overwhelmed, furious, and hurt. His anger combined with the amount of testosterone he was taking in such a way that he wanted badly to punch his pastor. The way Dave felt in that moment was the same way he felt when his family assaulted and disowned him. Just when he thought he had found a new family that loved and affirmed him, Dave realized that he was alone again.

Black and Gay Aren't Mutually Exclusive

Janice is a black woman who identifies as lesbian. She has been in a monogamous relationship with her partner for ten years. They are active in their small church, a racially mixed but predominantly black congregation with a dynamic pastor and rich social justice ministries. Janice has always had a deep commitment to her faith and, while she enjoys her career as a personal trainer, she has struggled with a calling to ministry for several years. She finds herself praying for her clients on a daily basis and has even prayed at the end of some tough training sessions with one or two of her clients who noticed how devout Janice is. One day, a client she had trained for several years paused midlunge and told her, "As good as you are at personal train-ing, I bet you'd be even better as a minister. You're always encouraging and supporting. Isn't that pretty much what a minister does?" Janice teased her client, assuming that he just wanted to quit doing lunges, but their conversa-tion deepened, and Janice truly began to realize that she was, indeed, called to ministry.

After a period of discernment, a lot of prayer with her partner, and some thoughtful conversations with her pastor, Janice decided to apply to semi-nary. Her application materials were strong, and she felt confident that she would be accepted to at least one of the seminaries on her list. Because she respected her pastor so much, Janice secretly had her heart set on attend-ing the seminary from which her pastor had graduated fifteen years prior. The seminary was theologically progressive, it affirmed women and LGBTQ persons in ministry, and it was racially diverse; all these factors contributed to Janice's desire to attend. She spoke with the dean of admissions by phone the day prior to her first visit to confirm all the details. Janice could not wait to meet the dean, to sit in on a class, and to encounter students who could become her classmates.

When Janice arrived at the admissions office, she was asked to be seated until the dean finished a phone call. Since she had arrived a few minutes early, Janice took the opportunity to gather her thoughts and breathe deeply; she was having a difficult time containing her excitement! The dean of admissions opened the door to her office and walked out. She looked around, made eye contact with Janice, looked around again, and walked back into her office. A few moments later, she came out with a file folder in her hand. Jan-ice noticed her own name printed neatly on the folder and shifted her weight in her seat, nervous that the dean was likely holding her application. The dean looked around the room again and said loudly, "Janice? Is Janice here for an admissions meeting?" Janice was befuddled. She glanced around the room. She and the dean were the only two people present in the room. The dean's assistant sat in the conjoined office. Janice raised her hand awkwardly and said, "I'm Janice." She rose and shook the dean's hand firmly.

The dean looked a bit bewildered and opened Janice's folder. She looked back at the application and then invited Janice into her office. The dean settled into her chair behind her desk and opened Janice's file once again. Janice noticed that it was opened to her application essay. Janice spent many days writing her essay, pouring her heart into words about her experiences reconciling her faith with her sexuality as a lesbian. It had been difficult for her and her family, but they all worked together and became even closer through her coming-out process. She wrote about the powerful role her pastor had in the process and how she felt called particularly to minister to the LGBTQ community. Janice remembered her passionate words and could sense the tension in the room. "Why does this feel so awkward?" she wondered to herself. "This seminary says on its website that it affirms LGBTQ people."

Being a bold and forthright person, Janice decided to cut through the tension and simply ask the dean why she seemed so confused about Janice's presence. The dean responded, "You wrote a beautiful application essay, explicitly naming that you're a lesbian. We have plenty of gays and lesbians here at our seminary, but all of them are white because the black church just isn't affirming of the gay lifestyle." Janice was completely taken aback. Janice knew plenty of other gay and lesbian Christians who were black; in fact, her church loved and affirmed them as members. She knew that some black churches didn't affirm homosexuality, but she also knew of a lot of white churches that didn't either. She didn't understand how the dean of admissions could make such a blanket stereotype. She tried hard to brush off the comment as her visit continued, but the more she thought about it, the more it troubled her.

When she returned home to tell her partner about her visit, she said, "This kind of thinking, that the black church doesn't accept gay people, was so entrenched in the dean's mind that she didn't even recognize that I was the applicant she was meeting with. Did she keep looking around because she thought she was supposed to be meeting with some white lesbian? Was she wondering what the heck this black woman was doing in her office?" Even though the seminary was at the top of her list, Janice simply couldn't shake this initial encounter. No matter how much the seminary's website communicated welcome and inclusion, Janice felt anything but welcomed and included when she visited.

Straight Privilege and Cisgender Privilege

In these two examples, Janice and Dave were hurt because of individual behavior stemming from straight privilege and cisgender privilege. Straight privilege refers to the unearned political, social, and economic advantages granted to heterosexuals based solely on their sexuality. These same advantages are routinely denied to LGBTQ persons. As previously indicated, an individual's access to such privileges is also impacted by race, ethnicity, gender, and ability. Cisgender privilege refers to the unearned political, social, and economic advantages granted to cisgender persons based solely on their gender identity. These same advantages are routinely denied to transgender persons. Because we live in a heteronormative society that adheres to strict male/female gender binaries, it is often quite difficult for straight and/or cisgender persons to acknowledge or realize that they are afforded privileges denied to LGBTQ persons. An overused example that is currently shifting in the United States is the right to marry. When most cisgender men and women get married, they are not aware that accompanying the signing of their marriage license is a vast array of federal rights denied to couples who cannot legally marry. The list is long, but other legal privileges afforded straight people and routinely denied LGBTQ folks include unquestioned access to a partner in medical facilities, joint-parent adoption, lack of discrimination in hiring or firing, paid employment leave upon the death of a spouse, or the ability to share health, auto, and homeowner's insurance. Additionally, many transgender people are unable to change the gender assigned at birth on their birth certificate. Cisgender people never have to worry that the document announcing their existence in the world does not match who they are. This impacts many other documents, such as a driver's license, a passport, and other forms of identification that require one to check "male" or "female."

In addition to legal privileges granted to straights and denied to LGBTQs, the dominant cultural messages portray straight families, heterosexual couples, and cisgender individuals as the norm. Straight cisgender people can turn on the television, attend a movie, or open a magazine and see myriad role models and reflections of themselves in popular culture. Oftentimes, LGBTQ people are either not portrayed or are depicted in a stereotypical or negative manner. A cisgender person never has to question which restroom to choose in public. Yet every time transgender people have to use the bathroom—a necessary and shared function among us all—they must question the consequences of their action. Because bathrooms, like clothing departments, are most often divided into "male" or "female," a transgender or genderqueer person who may not neatly fit into one of these binaries must risk harassment, violence, or at the very least, eye rolls, just to use the bathroom.

A straight person never has to announce his or her sexuality to family, friends, or acquaintances. Because of heteronormativity, everyone is assumed to be straight; being anything other than straight or cisgender is seen as straying from the norm. Consequently, when many LGBTQ people come out to friends, family, or acquaintances, they risk the loss of acceptance. Such was the case with Dave, whose family disowned him after he came out as transgender. The number of LGBTQ people who have been disowned by families is overwhelming. In addition to the loss of a relationship, some people become so angry at the coming out of an LGBTQ friend, family member, or acquaintance that they become physically violent. Even worse, LGBTQ people are victims of hate crimes, but in many states these assaults—even murders—are not treated as hate crimes because the particular state's discrimination laws do not include protection based on sexual orientation.[1] For these reasons, the rates of homelessness and suicide among LGBTQ persons are astronomical compared to those for straight and cisgender persons.[2] Worse, within the LGBTQ community, transgender individuals are maligned, misunderstood, and mistreated.

In our study of microaggressions in ministerial settings, it is not only legal and cultural privilege that is granted straight people—it is also theological privilege. Conservative churches, denominations, and seminaries adhering to a literal interpretation of the Bible assert that homosexuality is a sin and an abomination against God. Many of these same religious organizations believe that all LGBTQs are destined for hell. While many moderate churches, denominations, and seminaries may not blatantly say that LGBTQs are going to hell, some simply ignore the lives of LGBTQ people, thus contributing to the perpetuation of straight and cisgender privilege. Even many progressive churches, denominations, and seminaries that welcome and affirm LGBTQ people still hold up heterosexuality as the norm in polity, theology, and language. Virtually all churches—conservative, moderate, and liberal—often boldly and uncritically proclaim that "God made them male and female" from the creation narrative in Genesis. In the case of most conservative churches, this verse bolsters binary gender roles and procreation among only heterosexual couples. With moderate denominations, the Genesis account may be used to assert an egalitarian approach to the gender binary, yet it still excludes transgender and genderqueer people. And even many lesbian, gay, and bisexual liberal Christians may boldly read this Scripture, unaware of how damaging and hurtful it is to the transgender people in their presence.

Whether legal, cultural, or theological, straight and/or cisgender people are routinely afforded special privileges that LGBTQ persons cannot access. Since heteronormativity and traditional gender binaries are an everyday part of life, people who are lesbian, gay, bisexual, transgender, and queer encounter microaggressions that assault their souls on a routine basis.

Awareness: Recognizing LGBTQ Microaggressions in Ministry

Kevin Nadal's theoretical taxonomy of LGBT microaggressions is a very helpful tool for understanding the common forms of LGBTQ microaggressions.[3] Nadal names eight broad categories of microaggressive experience for LGBTQ people. Though Nadal's list is not exhaustive, it is a helpful beginning framework for churches and religious institutions aiming to address the hidden violence of microaggressions against LGBTQ people.

1. The use of heterosexist or transphobic terminology. This is probably the most obvious form of microaggression and typically falls into the subcategory of microassault, whereby persons use intentionally derogatory language toward an LGBTQ person (for example, slurs such as *faggot* or *dyke* or *shemale*) or make explicitly pejorative comments about LGBTQ people.[4] The intentional use of heterosexist and transphobic language is sometime paired with theological "justification" for the expression of hatred or disdain. At just about any gay pride event in any city in the United States, one can find religious representatives speaking these messages of LGBTQ disdain loudly and with great theological assurance.

It is helpful for LGBTQ-affirming faith communities to consider what type of emotional, psychological, and spiritual violence is perpetrated in society on a regular basis toward the LGBTQ people who may find a spiritual home in these communities. It may be helpful to return again to chapter 2 in order to revisit the ways narratives—religious and otherwise—provide the material out of which we come to know something about ourselves at a deep level and the ways these same narratives purport to put us in relation to others in society as well as to the Divine.

2. The endorsement of heteronormative or gender-normative culture and behaviors. These microaggressions occur when LGBTQ persons are expected to act heterosexual or cisgender or to behave in accordance with heterosexual or cisgender norms despite their LGBTQ identity. Nadal provides the examples of a straight person telling a gay person not to "act so gay" and of cisgender parents forcing their child to dress according to the child's birth sex.[5]

The microaggressive endorsement of heteronormative or cisgender assumptions within ministerial settings also occurs with regularity. Microinvalidations occur any time that churches and other institutions simply overlook the lived human experience of LGBTQ people in their midst. This occurs, for example, when a hiring committee fails to acknowledge that gay male employees should have the ability to take paternity leave, rather than proceeding on the false assumption that gay men do not desire or plan to have children. Another common example of an environmental microinvalidation occurs when church or institutional facilities do not include gender-neutral or unisex restrooms and thus do not acknowledge that gender identity and expression make the forced choice between male and female restrooms uncomfortable or impossible for some transgender or genderqueer people. In sermons and lessons, the unintentional endorsement of heteronormative or gender-normative culture or behavior is also quite common, for example, when messages about marriage or intimate relationships tacitly assume that these relationships are always and only between a man and a woman and fail to acknowledge that these relationships also occur between two men or two women. These microinvalidating messages occur with regularity even in open and affirming environments simply due to the cultural baggage of heteronormativity that influences our thinking and communication outside of our conscious awareness or intentionality.

3. *The assumption of a universal LGBTQ experience.* It is a very common experience among LGBTQ people for a friend, family member, or acquaintance to assume that *all* gay men or *all* lesbians or *all* transgender people are the same in some fundamental way—either by sharing a common life experience or by living out stereotyped traits, characteristics, or behaviors. Another form of this microaggression trope occurs when an LGBTQ person is asked to speak on behalf of other LGBTQ people about a supposed shared experience or perspective.[6] When we speak about the lived experience of LGBTQs from the pulpit or in the classroom, we must recognize the many ways our identities are multiply constituted not only by the intersection of factors such as our race, gender, class, sexual orientation, dis/ability, gender identity, nationality, and religion, but also by the unique narratives that comprise our singular subjective experience.

4. *The exoticization of LGBTQ experience.* Nadal explains this form of microaggressive experience in which LGBTQ people are "dehumanized or treated as objects," rather than as unique, individual human beings with a diversity of life experiences, preferences, and perspectives.[7] This can occur when LGBTQ people are stereotyped on television as the comic relief in a cast of characters, for example.[8] But this form of microaggression occurs with great regularity within explicitly LGBTQ-negative theological frameworks in which LGBTQ people are publicly portrayed as sexually deviant, as harboring the intention of "recruiting" young people, or as sexual predators of the young. Even an oversexualization of gay, lesbian, and bisexual people—representing sexual attraction and activity as the sole concern in our talk of LGBTQ lives—illustrates an exoticization microaggression. The experiences of transgender people are often microaggressively exoticized through asking inappropriate questions and making assumptions about their

process of transition and the appearance of their genitals, or through prying for details about their life prior to transition. This exoticization of transgender experience is clearly displayed in the inappropriate questions that were lodged about Dave's name prior to transition and by the pastor's blatantly asking Dave about the appearance of his genitals and for details regarding his transition surgery.

5. *Discomfort with or disapproval of LGBT experience.* It is, unfortunately, quite common for LGBTQ people to experience disrespectful treatment or even overt criticism for their LGBTQ identity.[9] Cisgender and heterosexual people, on the other hand, would not expect to experience any of these messages about their gender identity or sexual orientation in the same situations. Seminary or Sunday school classrooms and sermons are often fraught with these microaggressive messages.

For example, in a seminary class, three students out of seven in a small seminar engage in an impassioned denouncement of "homosexuals" based on a theological conviction of the sinfulness of homosexuality and a belief regarding its pathological nature. Other students are silent throughout the tirade. A bisexual male student, who is not out about his sexuality in the class, listens in anger and disbelief. He is unsure if he should voice his opposing views and worries about the possibility of outing himself in this hostile environment. He is still uncertain how the professor would regard him if he chooses to speak up in an LGBTQ-affirming manner or reveal information about his own sexual identity. This, again, illustrates the catch-22 of responding to microaggressions discussed in previous chapters, whereby confronting microaggressions can exacerbate the potential for further verbal or even physical violence.

While disrespectful or disapproving messages toward LGBTQ people are common in both church and wider society, an intensified power to harm attends these messages when couched within religious or theological language that purports to set life within a presumed ultimate context. Added theological weight justifies and intensifies LGBTQ denigration through appeal to sacred sources (e.g., Scripture) or to theological symbols and metaphors purporting to represent the mind and intention of God or, at very least, what is the only acceptable "orthodox" religious teaching on the matter. It becomes all the more important for leaders in communities of faith or religious and theological classrooms to attend to the potential for this type of theologically intensified microaggressive violence and to develop methods to intervene in ways that alleviate the catch-22 of responding for the LGBTQ people occupying these sacred or pedagogical spaces. These pastoral and pedagogical methods for responding to microaggression are the focus of the following three chapters.

6. Denial of the reality of heterosexism or transphobia. Churches and institutions that are intentionally welcoming of LGBTQ people and have adopted open and affirming positions in relation to LGBTQ persons in their communities and institutions must attend carefully to this form of microaggression. It is easy to fall into an inattentive posture when a community believes itself to have completed its work in becoming welcoming and affirming of all people. Ironically, communities that have done a great deal of work toward inclusivity and justice for LGBTQ people are often most at risk of perpetrating the microaggressive denial of heterosexism and transphobia. There are always ways that even the most progressive and inclusive individuals and communities of faith are unknowingly complicit in the continuation of LGBTQ injustice. Kneejerk denials of heterosexism and transphobia should always give us pause and serve as invitations to reconsider the ways we may unknowingly contribute to microaggressive communication.

7. The assumption of sexual pathology or abnormality for LGBTQ people. Nadal points to the ways that gay, lesbian, and bisexual people are portrayed as oversexualized or considered sexual deviants.[10] This is a common microassault in many situations in which an explicitly LGBTQ-denigrating theological framework is employed to speak of LGBTQ lives. Sermons and religious literature that portray gay and lesbian people as predators or that compare LGBTQ people to pedophiles are indicative of this type of pathologizing microassault. More subtly, microinsults are often perpetrated against LGBTQ people when it is assumed that every LGBTQ person struggles with depression or has contemplated or attempted suicide. While this represents the experience of some LGBTQ people, struggles with mental health concerns or suicide do not typify the experience of all LGBTQ persons. Within religious contexts, the presumption of LGBTQ "sinfulness" represents a theological way of pathologizing LGBTQ people and representing LGBTQ lives as spiritually abnormal. These theological representations have profound microaggressive effects (see chapter 2).

Churches that refuse the embrace of church membership or the rite of baptism to LGBTQ people communicate a microaggressive message that says, "You are inferior, subhuman, lesser beings." Another example of this type of assumption is the way religious representatives regularly speak of "LGBTQ people" and "Christians" as categories of persons that are mutually exclusive, as if one identity claim negates the other. The subtle, demeaning message communicates insensitivity to the reality that many LGBTQ persons *are* Christians and that the two groups are not mutually exclusive. Thus, the all-too-common ways that sermons, debates, and everyday speech present LGBTQ people as a category in contradistinction to Christian people subtly communicates a stereotype of LGBTQ persons as anti-Christian, which comes through to queer ears no matter the overt message that is intended. The message is not necessarily intended as directly hostile or aggressive. The speaker may not even be aware that the message is functioning in this insulting way. Nevertheless, it comes through as a microinsulting communication to those who are both Christian and LGBTQ, placing LGBTQ people in a category of theological abnormality in *opposition* to Christian values and commitments. The message is subtle and usually unintentional, but the microaggressive potential is profound.

8. The denial of individual heterosexism or transphobia.[11] This is a microaggressive communication by which cisgender or straight people fail to acknowledge their own heterosexist or cisgender biases and complicity in larger discourses and institutions that uphold heterosexual or cisgender privilege. Many lesbian, gay, and bisexual people are equally culpable in the perpetuation of cisgender privilege and deny their own transphobia by pointing to their involvement in LGBTQ activism without acknowledging that much of it fails to take seriously the lived experiences of transgender and genderqueer individuals.

Nadal also speaks of the intersections of LGBTQ microaggressions with racial microaggressions. These intersections occur in painful and damaging ways when racial-minority LGBTQ people experience exclusion within communities of color, when racial-minority LGBTQ people experience exclusion within LGBTQ groups, when the existence of racism is denied within LGBTQ communities, or when the existence of LGBTQ people is denied within communities of color.[12] This is well illustrated in the vignette of Janice, whose identity as a lesbian was not recognized in an LGBTQ-affirming seminary setting because of her racial identity.

Gay and bisexual men are not immune to enacting gender-oriented microaggressions against straight, lesbian, or bisexual women by drawing on unquestioned male privilege that exists within the wider society as well as within LGBTQ communities. It is also the case that LGB people have very often not sufficiently questioned their own internalized cisgender privilege and the ways that this privilege emerges in the enactment of microaggressions toward transgender and genderqueer people. Embodying one frequently targeted identity certainly does not make one immune from enacting microaggressions toward other embodiments of human difference.

Assessment: Understanding the Power of LGBTQ Microaggressions to Harm

The above theological contextualization of Nadal's theoretical taxonomy of LGBT microaggressions should help readers imagine the many ways these microaggressions occur in the daily experience of LGBTQ people in society as well as in religious and theological contexts. In religious contexts, the power of microaggressive violence to harm LGBTQ people is especially strong due to the theological intensification that is afforded to already quite strong and still fairly widespread social negativity toward LGBTQ people. For LGBTQ people living life in relation to a religious or spiritual tradition, theological words, narratives, and symbols inform our understanding of who we are as human beings, bringing into awareness our deepest sense of selfhood and weaving our multifaceted identities out of these linguistic and narratival threads. Religious language and symbols even attempt to move beyond personal and social descriptors to say something about the self's coreness, or soul, and our relationship to an ultimate context, or God.

Given the power of theologically intensified microaggressions to harm LGBTQ people at the depths of their being, churches and religious institutions aiming to cultivate a less microaggressive, more fully life-affirming atmosphere for LGBTQ people must take care to understand the complexities of potential harm. What is at stake in addressing microaggressions is far more than being politically correct. Instead, the *fundamental well-being of human lives* within our faith communities and religious institutions is our primary concern. Thus, we will address the potential harm of LGBTQ microaggressions under two broad categories: fragmentation of self and fragmentation of community.

Fragmentation of Self

In recent years, instances of LGBTQ suicide have gained intensified coverage in the mainstream news media, especially in the months following the September 2010 suicide of Rutgers student Tyler Clementi, which took place amid a spate of gay teenage suicides related to school bullying. While suicide is not ubiquitous among LGBTQ people—indeed, there are many LGBTQ people who live their entire lives without attempting or even contemplating suicide—suicide remains a matter of particular significance to those who are concerned for the well-being of LGBTQ people.

The U.S. Surgeon General's *2012 National Strategy for Suicide Prevention* names lesbian, gay, bisexual, and transgender populations as a specific group with increased suicide risk.[13] This publication reveals that between 12 to 19 percent of lesbian, gay, and bisexual adults reported making a suicide attempt in comparison to less than 5 percent of all U.S. adults. The statistics for adolescents are even more staggering, with at least 30 percent of LGBT adolescents reporting suicide attempts compared with 8 to 10 percent of all adolescents.[14] Looking specifically at the statistics for transgender persons, the 2011 National Transgender Discrimination Survey reveals that 41 percent of respondents reported a suicide attempt out of a total of 6,450 participants included in the study.[15]

While the reasons for these high suicide attempt rates are complex and multifaceted, the phenomenon of LGBTQ suicide is the most potent indicator of the potential damage done to the sense of self for LGBTQ people. While this damage has many originating sites (e.g., family rejection, peer rejection and bullying, hostile institutional environments, legal discrimination), both larger anti-LGBTQ theological frameworks and more-subtle religiously fueled microaggressions must be named in any examination of the harm done against the LGBTQ self. Thus, we ask what role religious and theological language, narrative, and symbol play in informing a sense of self for LGBTQ people, making suicide a thinkable option at much higher rates than for straight and cisgender people, and what lessons we stand to learn in our religious institutions and faith communities.

Sue notes the pressure that denigrating social messages exert on LGBTQ people to separate their LGBTQ identity from their sense of self because of internalized prejudice. While internalized prejudice may stem from the everyday heterosexist and cisgender privilege LGBTQ people experience in society more broadly, for our purposes, we must consider how theological language and symbols augment this experience of prejudice by intensifying social prejudice, placing it within the context of ultimacy and adding layers of theological justification. From this perspective, the most penetrating violence of these communications comes not from surface-level microaggressive communication but from their citation of larger religious and social messages that denigrate LGBTQ people. For example, behind any microaggressive communication against LGBTQ people in religious spaces is a much larger theological framework that has consistently positioned LGBTQ lives on the disparaged side of the good/evil binary and on the underside of theological hierarchies of value and worth attributed to human lives. These queer-denigrating messages mark the LGBTQ body as an appropriate target for acts of insult, hatred, and violence. They occupy LGBTQ minds with the unsettling knowledge that always and everywhere, LGBTQ persons are liable to become victims of violent attack just for bringing their sexuality or gender identity to light.

Overt microassaults (e.g., "fag") hurled at LGBTQ people can operate as even more insidious citations of social and religious portrayals of the LGBTQ self as sick, sinful, or an object of disgust and derision. These images swirl in social consciousness without need of explicit mention in order for the citation to become evident. Social-religious discourses experienced both directly and as ambient messages in the social milieu provide available material out of which LGBTQ people come to construct a sense of self. Often encountered very early in life, these messages become part of the lens through which LGBTQ people develop a sense of their own core identity, or soul.

Even when an LGBTQ person consciously disavows messages that being LGBTQ means somehow being sick or sinful, these discourses nevertheless become a part of the constitutive material of the soul; they are building blocks taken up from the social context and used to construct a core sense of self for LGBTQ people. The problem ensues when some of these building blocks contain messages that a particular aspect of the self is bad, disordered, or sinful and should be broken off or kept hidden or separate from the rest. Noting the pressures to fragment or compartmentalize an LGBTQ identity from one's sense of self, Sue has this to say:

> Fragmentation or compartmentalization of the self results in feelings of isolation, alienation, and a possible sense of existential unreality about one's identity. According to this view, the conflict is between a need to perceive oneself as a good, moral and worthwhile person, contrasted against the belief that being gay or lesbian is immoral, indecent, and repugnant. . . . Internal separation and distancing become the psychological maneuvers that allow the lesbian and gay person to maintain their sense of "goodness," although this is often experienced as inauthentic and false.[16]

In addition to fragmentation and compartmentalization of an LGBTQ identity from one's sense of self, Sue argues that a process of identity denigration often occurs, which is akin to what might be commonly called self-hatred. He posits that when LGBTQ persons are deeply aware of their own sexual orientation or gender identity as an important part of their sense of identity or being, a sense of guilt can ensue "that represents recognition of self-denigration and the existence of undesirable attributes in the self. Both *threat and guilt* are constant and continuing experiences of internalized prejudice."[17] When one adds to the socially denigrating discourses on LGBTQ identities an additional layer of theological justification that suggests that the undesirability of LGBTQ sexuality or gender identity is embedded within the orthodox theological view of human personhood or, indeed, that it emerges from the very mind of God, the potential for identity denigration or self-hatred is greatly exacerbated.

Didier Eribon illustrates Sue's argument concerning the presence of threat and guilt in relation to these socially and religiously circulating denigrating messages:

The long-term effects of insult and hatred . . . write themselves into the body; they act by way of your own submission to the injunction that they carry, your own consent to the order they enforce—that your personality and your desires must remain hidden, that the line must be toed. They command you always to act "as if." They necessitate a permanent effort to ensure that none of your emotions, feelings, or desires are ever revealed.[18]

While overt heterosexism and genderism operate in insulting and hateful ways, microaggressions hold the potential to subtly carry forth the message of insult and hatred in ways that slip below the awareness of perpetrators. Despite the unintentionality of microaggressions, the messages continue to "write themselves into the body" of LGBTQs, perpetuating dynamics of self-fragmentation, identity denigration, and theologically intensified soul violence against LGBTQ lives.

Iris Marion Young sums up these oppressive dynamics this way: "The oppression of violence consists not only in direct victimization, but in the daily knowledge shared by all members of oppressed groups that they are *liable* to violation, solely on account of their group identity."[19] Indeed, when left unaddressed, the presence and potential of microaggressions in religious and ministerial environments continue to cultivate an environment where the mere likelihood of microaggressive violence upholds a communal culture of fragmentation, hiding, and fearful communication. Not only does leaving LGBTQ microaggressions unaddressed harm individuals, however; ultimately, it is also harmful to communities of faith.

Fragmentation of Community

One of the greatest harms to genuine community comes in the tacit injunction that microaggressive speech issues to hide important parts of oneself from others in order to be included as a valued part of the community. Even amid increasing visibility in the media, gains in LGBTQ rights, and increasing inclusion into the full life of churches and denominations, many churches and religious institutions maintain either explicit or implicit "don't ask, don't tell" policies regarding LGBTQ identities. These policies create microinvalidating environments for LGBTQ people and contribute to the fragmentation of authentic community in our faith traditions.

For example, a lesbian student who is not out about her sexuality in her seminary setting discovers that a fellow student who has been heard on many occasions making hostile remarks about LGBTQ people is going to be in a class with her the following semester. Fearful of what this experience might hold for her, the lesbian student decides to drop the class and change to a different section of the course, as she doesn't feel safe with this particular student in the classroom. Thus, the potential richness afforded by embodiments of human difference represented in the pedagogical space is self-selectively decreased because of a student's legitimate concern for her own emotional and spiritual well-being. Similarly, in the vignette of Janice, even though the seminary was at the top of her list, Janice simply couldn't shake her initial encounter with the dean of admissions, who wasn't able to understand how Janice could embody both black and lesbian identities. Janice will most likely move on to consider other seminaries instead.

In considering how environmental microaggressions shape communities of faith and learning, we must attend to concerns of *proxemics*, the physical arrangement of our bodies in relation to others, and *haptics*, the use of physical touch, and how these cues can operate in microaggressive ways toward LGBTQ people. Both casual touch and the arrangement of our selves in relation to others is often noticeably different when, for instance, instead of being in the presence of known heterosexual peers, a heterosexual man is with a gay or bisexual man. The heterosexual microaggressor may unconsciously communicate microinsults by withholding casual physical touch (e.g., a pat on the back or a hug) that is otherwise shared with heterosexual male peers. This may also occur through subtle but noticeable physical distancing (e.g., empty chairs between a heterosexual student and a gay student in the classroom). This is a subtle and perhaps unintentional citation of a larger social and theological discourse of disgust in relation to LGBTQ lives.[20] The gay student in this example is left to wonder whether microaggressive haptics and proxemics involving the regulation of touch and physical proximity are, indeed, based on his peers' perception of his sexual identity. More difficult, the enactor of these potentially microaggressive proxemics may be unaware that his physical actions are influenced by knowledge of his peer's sexual orientation.

In all of these examples, the moment of microaggressive experience may increase the targeted person's vigilance in response to the microaggression and lead to a process of internal deliberation to determine if the recipient's identity as an LGBTQ person is being attacked or whether the communication is a simple misunderstanding. The choice a recipient faces is either to accept the microaggressive experience as a simple reality of life for an LGBTQ person or to enact a confrontation of the perpetrator. Sue argues, "The internal struggle with microaggressions can fester and eat away at the integrity of the person for long periods of time."[21] The recipient may experience feelings of anger, anxiety, guilt, depression, and a host of other affective responses. Over time, the chronicity of microaggressive experience can wear down the targeted individuals, leading to experiences of exhaustion through the persistent confrontation of a hostile and invalidating climate that demands one comply with dominant experiences and expressions of reality by accepting the demeaning of one's self-esteem, the precariousness of one's personal psychological and physical safety, and the devaluing of one's lived experience.[22] These circumstances make the cultivation of genuine community nearly impossible.

Indeed, one's engagement in the life of community—whether in a local congregation or a seminary classroom—is affected by the tacit injunction for identity fragmentation and hiding. This dynamic not only diminishes the lives of some within these faith and learning communities, but it also diminishes the richness of communication that could otherwise take place within these worship and pedagogical spaces. Ultimately, in both "don't ask, don't tell" environments and institutional spaces where microaggressions are simply left unaddressed, the community is fragmented from within in ways that may not even be noticeable to those unwilling to question the taken-for-granted acceptance of the oppressive status quo. Increasing a community's willingness and skillfulness to address the presence and potential of LGBTQ-based microaggressions promotes the healing and repair of the self- and community-fragmentation that results from Christian churches' long and lingering history of denigrating LGBTQ people.

Action: Cultivating Religious Communities of Resistance and Resilience

Homiletics scholar Lucy Atkinson Rose encourages ministers to attend carefully to the implications of language in the lives of their congregants: "When personal experiences are validated and encouraged, not discounted or ridiculed, worshipers begin to risk listening to and articulating the sounds deep within their own hearts, even the echoes and memories of abuse and pain."[23] For LGBTQ people, the memories of abuse and pain are extensive, extending beyond individual memory to a collective cultural and religious memory of abuse and pain inflicted against faithful queer people from age to age. In order to honor and validate, rather than discount and ridicule, the lived human experiences of religious abuse and spiritual pain, religious institutions and communities of faith must develop the conceptual and linguistic framework to speak openly and honestly about the perpetuation and exacerbation of these experiences through microaggressive communication that flies under the radar of many good, liberal, LGBTQ-affirming congregations. The rest of this chapter includes a few simple suggestions to begin the development of this framework for constructively engaging LGBTQ-based microaggressions within these ministerial contexts.

First, it is imperative for us to recognize that heterosexual and cisgender privilege is often communicated most clearly by what we *don't* say. Silence on sexual orientation and gender identity is a common microinvalidating experience within religious contexts. Lives that fall outside of the dominant, normative framework for understanding human experience—in this case a straight and cisgender status quo—are negated through a systematic erasure from speech. A common example occurs when a list of human differences is given in a church's welcome statement (e.g., "We welcome people of all races, classes, genders . . ."). It is a noticeable message of unwelcome when one's own marker of human difference is left out of such a list. In a religious milieu where LGBTQ exclusion is still pervasive, churches have to work even harder to communicate that LGBTQ people are truly embraced into the full life of the community.[24] In churches wishing to cultivate an affirming space for LGBTQ people, simply hearing the words *lesbian, gay, bisexual,* and *transgender* spoken in positive, affirming ways from the pulpit and in other means of communication can be important—even when the minister or congregation believes this affirmation is implied.

Second, in considering the experience of transgender, intersex, and genderqueer persons within religious contexts, setting the stage for intentional and ongoing conversation about gendered language is crucial. As we have seen, the notion that "God made them male and female" from the creation narrative in Genesis can set a theological barrier to imagining life beyond the gender binary. We must, however, continue to cultivate our theological imaginations by reading this text and others in light of the lived human experience of transgender, intersex, and genderqueer people and even in light of other biblical texts, such as Galatians 3:28: "there is no longer male and female." Developing our capacity for language is not only a concern for speech in public spaces such as classrooms and sanctuaries, but also in one-to-one communication. Here, pronoun usage becomes an essential topic of conversation, as it is not always clear to minds shaped by a cultural acquiescence to the male/female gender binary just which pronoun a person prefers or whether a person has adopted a gender-neutral pronoun such as *ze* rather than *he* or *she*.[25]

If in doubt about the importance of this concern, recall the vignette in which a fellow member in an LGBTQ support group began to nag Dave incessantly about what his "real name" was. The gay member was referring to the name given to Dave at birth, a name typically assigned to a girl. Dave knew there was nothing constructive the member could do with his birth name and wanted to move past that part of his life and live fully into his authentic self: Dave, a man. Another member kept insisting that Dave and his female partner were in a lesbian relationship because Dave was "biologically female." Dave felt invalidated, as though the person clearly didn't acknowledge the difference between being lesbian (a sexual orientation) and being trans (a gender identity). Experiences like this one are commonplace for transgender people, even in religious contexts that set out to welcome and affirm LGBTQ people.

Finally, churches and other religious institutions must broaden ways of comprehending and speaking about embodiment and identity. Theologian Patrick Cheng foregrounds the notion of *multiplicity* as a vital element in our continued dialogue on human difference, defining the term as "a state of having multiple co-existing and overlapping identities, as opposed to a singular dominant identity."[26] The multiplicity of our identities touches on our experience and embodiment of race, gender, sexuality, gender identity, class, nationality, dis/ability, and a host of other markers of human difference.

Cheng notes the important experience of "middle-space existence," which is especially pertinent for LGBTQ people of color, who are caught between binary poles of race and sexuality.[27] For example, Janice experienced the microaggressive bifurcation of her race and sexual identity in ways that imposed on her a middle-space existence in which the fullness of her humanity was not acknowledged in a way that honored the multiple identities vital to her embodied experience. Cheng speaks of theological practices of *mediation* "bringing together sources, voices, and perspectives that are normally not seen as belonging together."[28] This includes bringing together the multiplicity of our identities (race, sexuality, gender, class, gender identity, religion, nationality, dis/ability, etc.) in ways that acknowledge and honor the ways these "identities" are not discrete markers of difference but that are "mutually co-constituted"—interplaying in a variety of complex ways.[29] By making our conceptual frameworks, theological narratives, and linguistic tools for understanding and communicating about our human experience more complex, we expand both imaginations and vocabularies in ways that resist microaggressive violence within congregations and other religious institutions. In so doing, the resilience of parishioners and students can develop, along with their capacity to constructively resist microaggressive violence in their everyday lives.

PART 3   Microaggressions in
          Ministerial Practice

Chapter 6

Microaggressions in Word

Preaching and Education

A Woman's Place Behind the Pulpit

Sienna Gomez was ordained twenty-five years ago. Throughout her tenure as an ordained clergywoman, she has served as a chaplain, associate pastor, and senior pastor. Because she loves preaching, she enjoys being a senior pastor most; Sienna thrives when researching, writing, and delivering a sermon. She views preaching as an opportunity to learn more about Scripture each week and to share this knowledge with her congregation so that they can deepen their relationships with God.

Along the way, Sienna has honed the craft of preaching and become a skilled orator. She has even received a few preaching awards and has had five of her sermons published in various books and periodicals. Her preaching has been described as dynamic, inspirational, engaging, thoughtful, and prophetic. In most sermons, she causes congregants to both laugh and cry, in addition to challenging them to think about faith in new and creative ways. In brief, Sienna is a stellar preacher who is well respected within her denomination and community.

She knew when she was ordained twenty-five years ago that she would face challenges as a preacher because of her gender. She often jokes with other female colleagues, "If I had a dollar for every time someone told me I was the 'best *woman* preacher' they've ever heard,' I'd be a millionaire!" In these ways, Sienna is accustomed to dealing with gender-related microaggressions from the pulpit. Over time, she has developed strategies for coping with the sexism in comments like these. In fact, in recent years Sienna has noticed some shifts in responses to her preaching and has begun to wonder whether the tides are changing for women preachers.

Due to the respect she has gained throughout her denomination, Sienna has been invited to be one of the preachers at a three-night revival in another state. On the evenings when the preachers are not preaching, they will pray, read Scripture, and take on additional leadership roles in worship. Sienna is excited about the revival and prepares diligently so that she can craft a thoughtful sermon. She is slated to preach on the second evening. On the first and third evenings, both preachers are male. Sienna is not surprised by this, as she is often the only woman in leadership represented at denominational gatherings.

When Sienna and her two male colleagues arrive at the church, they are greeted by the church's senior pastor. Charlie has served this church for nearly thirty years and is beloved by the congregation. Both Charlie and the congregation value women in ministry, have participated in ordaining quite a few women over the years, and even have two women pastors on staff. Charlie and the three guest preachers discuss details related to preaching and divide up leadership roles in worship. Charlie notes that his church has a split chancel; the preaching is done from the pulpit, which is larger and lifted higher, and all other speaking during worship occurs from the lectern. On the raised chancel are three chairs with pockets for holding Bibles and hymnals.

That evening, Charlie and the three guest preachers assemble outside of the sanctuary for prayer. As the organ begins the prelude, the four clergy line up to process into the sanctuary. Sienna is last in line. As they approach the chancel, Sienna assumes that the three guest preachers will sit in the three chairs on the raised platform and that Charlie will sit on the front pew. Instead, Charlie leads the two men onto the chancel, and the three of them sit in the chairs. Sienna stands awkwardly in front of the chapel before deciding she should simply sit on the first pew. "I'm not preaching tonight; it's not that big of a deal," she thinks, even though she is frustrated to see only male faces on the platform. As worship begins, Charlie walks to the pulpit and introduces the guest preacher for the evening, mentioning his preaching accomplishments and degrees and noting that "he lives with his wife and two children in Indiana." The community worshiped. The guest preacher preached. It was a fine evening.

The next evening, the four clergy gather again for prayer outside the sanctuary. Sienna considers mentioning the unequal seating arrangement but decides it is unnecessary since she is preaching that evening. The four clergy process in again with Sienna last in line. Again, the three male clergy ascended the chancel and leave Sienna to sit in the front pew. Sienna feels her temperature rise. "Why is this bothering me so much?" she wonders. "I know Charlie and this church value women in ministry, but I'm really feeling overlooked." Charlie walks to the pulpit to introduce Sienna and, unlike the previous evening, he does not mention any of Sienna's preaching awards or publications. In fact, Charlie fails to mention her ordination or that she is senior pastor of a church. Instead, he says, "Sienna is a great lady preacher! She is also a wonderful wife and mother. In fact, both her sons play basketball, just like mine."

Sienna hangs her head as she sits in the first pew, confused by why her introduction had little to do with preaching and ministry and everything to do with her role as a wife and mother. When the time comes for Sienna to preach, Charlie stands to read Scripture as Sienna approaches the chancel. Out of habit, Charlie walks to the pulpit. Sienna stands awkwardly between the pulpit and the lectern, assuming she will walk to the pulpit once Charlie finishes because that's where all the preaching takes place. Instead, as Charlie completes the Gospel reading, he gestures for Sienna to stand behind the lectern. In that moment, Sienna is furious. She has already been treated differently from the men in her seating and introduction, and now she is being relegated to the lectern rather than the pulpit, as though her sermon is less valuable than those of her male colleagues. She doesn't want to cause a scene in the middle of the revival, so she steps up to the lectern and delivers one of the best sermons of her career.

When worship ends and the clergy recess out, Charlie thanks Sienna for an inspiring sermon. "You sure can preach!" he tells her. The other guest preachers agree enthusiastically. "Then why did you treat me differently from the men preaching?" she asks Charlie angrily. Charlie was taken aback. "What are you talking about, Sienna?"

"Two nights in a row, there wasn't one woman seated on the chancel. I'm one of the preachers, and I had to sit on the front row instead of with all the other clergy. When you introduced my male colleagues, you told everyone about their ministerial accomplishments. When you introduced me—the lone clergywoman—you talked about how my sons play basketball! And the cherry on top is that I preached from the lectern. The lectern! You even told us that the sermons are reserved for the pulpit and that all other spoken words come from the lectern. Yet when the time came for the only female pastor present to preach, I had to preach behind the lectern while you read Scripture from the pulpit!" Sienna surprised herself—and Charlie—with the anger in her voice. It was as though all the frustration stemming from battling sexism was spilling out in this moment. She blushed and felt a mixture of shame and fury. There was an extremely awkward moment of silence. Charlie and Sienna stared at each other in disbelief as the two other clergy stood with their mouths agape.

"Oh my God, Sienna. I had no idea. I mean, I didn't realize. You were last in line. I didn't think about it. Your kids are great basketball players. What I mean is that, I walked to the pulpit out of habit; I've been doing it for thirty years. I just . . ." Charlie rambled. "Sienna, I am so sorry," Charlie finally managed. "You truly are one of the best preachers I've ever heard—male or female. I never intended to treat you differently. I didn't even notice any of the things you mentioned."

"That's because you don't have to notice, Charlie. Everywhere you look you see people who look like you," Sienna responded, calmly, but firmly.

"You're absolutely right," said Charlie fervently. "I cannot believe I did this. I can see completely why you're so angry. I don't even have to think about these things as a man, but you have to battle sexism all the time as a woman in ministry. Geez, I can only imagine what kind of message I was sending to all the women in my congregation. I'm sure it looked like I thought the guys were more important than you. I don't think that at all. That wasn't what I meant. I have to make this right." He genuinely could not believe his actions. He felt so embarrassed. "Sienna, I know you've had a long night, and I don't want to ask more from you, but can we talk about this a little more?"

Sienna agreed, and they shared a good conversation. It was good primarily because Charlie chose to listen while Sienna told him what it was like to be a woman preacher. Instead of spouting everything he had learned or read or even claimed to believe about the importance of women in ministry, Charlie knew that his role needed to be that of a listener.

The next evening, Sienna led the three male clergy during the processional and was seated on the platform while Charlie took his place in the first pew. When Charlie ascended the steps to the lectern to introduce the guest preacher for the evening, he took a few moments to apologize and to share with the congregation how he had implicitly behaved in sexist ways over the past two nights of the revival. "We are a congregation that prides ourselves for valuing women in ministry, but my actions did not reflect this value over the last two nights. Instead, I behaved out of habit, routine, and never even considered how my actions were impacting women. For this I am truly sorry." Charlie also called a special meeting with his preaching and worship planning committee so that they could hold one another accountable for creating spaces of equality and inclusion in worship and preaching from that point forward.

Privilege and Confusion: Taking Responsibility

Pastor James is a middle-aged white man who has served a diverse congregation for nearly ten years. An urban congregation with about 200 people in worship each Sunday, the church is filled with robust educational ministries.

Sunday school classes and special topics classes are filled with congregants and community members from an array of ages, socioeconomic classes, races, genders, sexual orientations, and ethnicities. The church and Pastor James pride themselves in the ways they embody the notion of the beloved community on earth.

A sizable group within the congregation wanted a class that would explore the ways in which different texts and works of art from around the world portrayed Jesus. Pastor James loved the idea and was grateful that he had taken a class on a similar topic in seminary. He spent several months gathering the materials and preparing for the class while the congregation drummed up interest within the church and community.

At the first meeting, Pastor James and many congregational leaders were thrilled at the number of people in attendance. Many members were there, and so were quite a few new visitors. Some of the people in the class had never read any of the Gospels, and some were professors of religion. In the first few classes, the participants discussed feminist and womanist theology and their depictions of Jesus, the faces of Jesus throughout Africa, and the way Jesus is portrayed in black liberation theology.

Pastor James opened the class on Jesus in Latin American liberation theology with a prayer written by Archbishop Oscar Romero. He went on to spend most of the class discussing the way Jesus is portrayed in Peru, utilizing much of Gustavo Gutiérrez's work. Throughout the class, Pastor James quoted Gutiérrez, described the basic tenants of his theology, and even displayed his photograph. At least he *thought* he displayed Gutiérrez's photograph on the projector. Instead, Pastor James displayed a photograph of Leonardo Boff. Further, every time Pastor James quoted Gutiérrez, he attributed the quote to Boff. He even discussed what it was like for Boff to be a theologian in Peru. Boff, however, is a liberation theologian from Brazil.

At the end of the class, Pastor James was approached by a visitor who had attended every class but was not a member of the church. She told him how much she had enjoyed the first three sessions of the class but that this evening's session had troubled her. She told him that many of the quotes he had read and stories he had shared were not from Boff but from Gutiérrez. "You showed a photo of Boff and talked about how his theology was liberating for fellow Peruvian people, but Boff is from Brazil. You were actually talking about the work of Gutiérrez. They are two different men from two entirely different countries; not all Latinos are the same, you know."

At first Pastor James pushed back. "Are you sure?" he asked the visitor. "You know I took a class on this in seminary." The woman looked a bit angry but simply nodded her head. Pastor James opened his mouth, intent on showing how much research he had done to prepare for the class and how he would never make such a mistake. Because he pastors a diverse congregation that teaches classes in English as a second language, he thought about how there's no way he could consider all Latino men to be the same. He was offended that this visitor would accuse him of making a seemingly racist mistake like this. Before he said a word, however, he decided to take a deep breath and consider the perspective of the woman talking with him.

After his deep breath, Pastor James realized he had made a pretty big mistake. He felt embarrassed and didn't really know what to say to the woman. He feared that he would appear racist. He wanted to defend himself, rationalize his mistake, or brush it off as no big deal. Instead, he looked the visitor in the eye and said, "I'm very sorry. Are you in a hurry to leave or do you have a moment to chat?" The woman was a bit surprised by his seemingly sudden change in demeanor and decided to give Pastor James a chance to explain himself.

Pastor James admitted his mistake and apologized for it. "I'm a white man, and there isn't a long history of people oppressing white men. I'm so proud of the fact that I pastor a diverse community; it's really important to me. But just because it's important to me doesn't mean I don't make mistakes. And I made a big one. I wanted to just brush it off when you first brought it up; I know this reaction comes from my own privilege, and I am truly sorry. If it's acceptable to you, I plan to begin class next week by apologizing for my mistake. Is this okay with you?"

Though it did not change the fact that Pastor James had done something microaggressively racist in class, the woman was grateful that he accepted responsibility for his actions and was taking steps to address their ramifications. Pastor James did as he promised and told the class about his mistake. While doing so, he felt embarrassed and awkward, but he kept reminding himself that the woman who corrected him must have felt worse. He displayed the correct photograph and took his blunder as an opportunity to talk a bit about privilege in class; instead of teaching the class about privilege, Pastor James opened the floor for people to share their own experiences. Several people from different minority groups talked about being mistaken for someone else within their particular group and how hurtful and invalidating this felt. After the session ended, several persons of color addressed Pastor James separately and thanked him for taking responsibility for his actions. A few white male congregants told him that this session opened their eyes to some of their own privileges. Pastor James thanked the visiting woman again and committed to being more thoughtful, reflective, and careful in the future.

Constructive Tools for Addressing Microaggressions
in Preaching and Education

A focus on the ethics of language use in the literature of homiletics and religious education is certainly not novel.[1] It is helpful at the outset to note a few particular strands in the homiletics literature that are illustrative of a broad ethos in the field into which our treatment of microaggressions in preaching may be situated. In her construction of a "conversational" model of preaching, Lucy Atkinson Rose cites key figures in twentieth-century homiletics who foreground the limitations of language and the potential that all language holds to perpetuate the conditions of particular historical, political, and social settings.[2] One such homiletician, Robert E. C. Browne, warned preachers of the inherent ambiguity in language use and the inability to conceive of words as unchanging entities with precise referents.[3] While not precluding the use of language about "truth," Browne believed that any truth communicated must always remain ambiguous. Rose points to a second exemplary homiletics scholar in Joseph Sittler. Sittler pointed preachers to an awareness of language's historical, social, and political situatedness, further troubling any notion of direct correspondence between "reality" and language.[4]

Rose builds on these midcentury homiletical theorists to argue further that "all language, including the language of faith, is inevitably biased and limited, historically conditioned, and inseparable from the sins of each generation and each community of users."[5] This important reminder to preachers and teachers wishing to turn their attention to microaggressions points to the potential for violence and the perpetuation of oppressive ideology in all language use—perhaps *especially* in preaching and religious teaching. This elevated risk of linguistic, discursive violence in preaching is illustrated well in Rose's summarization of the work of Thomas Mickey's homiletical theory: "Preaching, [Mickey] claims, involves power because it participates in expressing, defining, and creating the community's identity and social order."[6]

A further concern for the potential of language to perpetuate violence against minority groups emerges from feminist-informed homiletics. Rebecca Chopp speaks of the "ordering of systems and consciousness that uncovers the relations, the anonymous rules, the hidden principles in language, subjectivity, and politics" that saturate preaching.[7] She calls theologians and preachers to a serious analysis of the potential for language to either uphold or resist dominant social-symbolic orders that adversely affect the lives of those whose voices are marginalized by these orders. She encourages those who work with language in the arts of ministry to take seriously the need for transformation of linguistic practices that uphold relations of domination, oppression, and violence:

> I do think transformation is necessary; for modern linguistic practices and discourses, which reflect and contribute to subjectivity and politics, do not allow for otherness, specificity, difference, solidarity, and transformation. Until we change the values and hidden rules that run through present linguistic practices, social codes, and psychic orderings, women, persons of color, and other oppressed groups will be forced—by the language, discourses, and practices available to them—into conforming to ongoing practices, to babbling nonsense, or to not speaking at all.[8]

Christine Smith echoes Chopp's feminist critique of preaching's perpetuation of oppressive ordering systems and the necessity of homiletical resistance: "Naming this web of oppression as the expression of radical evil has everything to do with preaching."[9]

A similar concern for the power of language to marginalize the other is evident in the deconstructive homiletics of John McClure. McClure's "otherwise preaching" is a form of homiletics "motivated and sustained by an *ethical* concern to reorient preaching toward the 'other,' to situate preaching as a radical act of compassionate responsibility."[10] Deconstructionist philosophy, particularly that of Emmanuel Levinas and Jacques Derrida, informs McClure's investigation into the potential for language to construct the worlds that we inhabit as well as the potential for preaching to deconstruct the language that serves to marginalize and subject others to discursive forms of violence and the oppressive ordering of social relations. The same is certainly true when it comes to the language of religious education.

Endeavoring to encourage preachers to attend carefully to the implications of language in the lives of their own congregants, Rose adds, "When personal experiences are validated and encouraged, not discounted or ridiculed, worshipers begin to risk listening to and articulating the sounds deep within their own hearts, even the echoes and memories of abuse and pain."[11] Attending carefully to the charge of these homileticians means taking seriously the admonition to view language as having less correspondence to "reality" and having far more to do with the construction of "realities" and the identities that so often become sites of marginalization and violence. This invites preachers and teachers into careful examination of the operative assumptions that rest just behind the words we speak in the pulpit and classroom, as our language is not simply communicating knowledge and ideas but is actively constructing the worlds that we inhabit, setting limits on the ability of others to find a place in those worlds.

If preachers and religious educators begin to recognize the ways that the theologically intensified effects of microaggressions cause deep harm to congregants and students, a double challenge is posed to those wishing to constructively address microaggressions in classroom and congregation. First, by their very nature, microaggressions persistently escape easy detection and overt critique. As we've discussed, their power rests in their invisibility to perpetrators ("I didn't say that!") and in their ambiguity to the ears of targeted recipients ("Did I really just hear that? Did they really *mean* that?"). Second, microaggressions communicate denigrating messages as citations of dominant social narratives on human difference, making them difficult to address critically and constructively. Indeed, Sue notes, "the most frequent reaction to microaggressions seems to be doing nothing."[12] If we wish to create religious communities that honor and respect all, doing nothing is simply unacceptable. So what pedagogical interventions can we make in hopes of decreasing the potential for microaggressive violence in our preaching and teaching?

First, in homiletics classrooms—where seminary students begin to learn the art of preaching—an agreement may be arrived on early in the course to treat in-class communications—intentional and unintentional—with open, critical but generous conversation. That means acknowledging our willingness to talk openly about microaggressions before they ever occur and preparing ourselves and our students to do so. We must all acknowledge our potential to engage in microaggressive speech, but to do so with the understanding that the classroom is a liminal space offering the potential for communicating *about* our communication in ways that help us become more attentive to our subtle slips of unintended insult, invalidation, and assault. This same type of agreement can be made among members of a Sunday school or religious education class once awareness is raised about the reality and potential harm of microaggressions.

In making such a classroom agreement or covenant, instructors should help students to understand the differences between policing "politically incorrect" language and the more difficult—but far more important—job of attending to the ways that microaggressions that operate with the force of religious or theological language, symbols, metaphors, and narratives take on an intensified ability to harm. The difference between "political correctness" and an ethical commitment to attend to language is seen in McClure's distinction between a "therapeutic" concern for abuses and misuses of power and "the use of more ethically oriented language" by which "the preacher begins to locate the seat of abusive hegemony less in idiosyncratic misuses of authority than in prevailing traditions, ontologies, language games, and identities themselves."[13] It is the latter, ethical attention to language that is our primary concern in teaching and preaching rather than a tepid, "therapeutic" scrupulous avoidance of offense by cautious use of politically correct language.

For example, while *homosexual* is no longer the politically correct designation in professional and academic communication about same-sex attraction, simply correcting a student's word usage forfeits an opportunity for greater attention to the power of language to define reality and construct identity. Instead of a mere language correction (e.g., "Please say *gay* instead of *homosexual*), intentional communication about language in the classroom allows for a more robust discussion of the potential for language to insert others into a field of meaning that operates in ways that marginalize lived experience and demean others based on embodiments of human difference. This occurrence could prompt important discussions about the etymological invention of the term and concept *homosexual*, which has been employed in medical and psychological discourse throughout recent history to pathologize same-sex sexuality and criminalize homosexual acts as socially deviant. The usage of *homosexual* continues to be used in denigrating ways among religious figures whose insistent refusal to acknowledge self-chosen linguistic descriptors for embodiments of human difference is a linguistic form of violence that prefigures other more insidious acts of psychological, spiritual, and even physical violence against LGBTQ persons. Thus, rather than a simple substitution for a more politically correct term, an instructor may help students to consider what larger social discourses their language is upholding — perhaps in ways they never intended.

As Sue argues, "Recognizing microaggressions when they make their appearance is more than an intellectual exercise in definitions. Their manifestations are dynamic, with very real personal consequences that can only be ameliorated when recognized in their interactional or environmental forms."[14] Homiletics classrooms — where language is the privileged subject — hold great potential as spaces for the training of student ministers to recognize microaggressive violence in the interactional dynamics of the classroom and in parallel dynamics within congregations.

While microaggressions are an appropriate pedagogical concern in any classroom, microaggressions education in the theological school offers the opportunity to engage in an examination of the racial, gender, sexual, and gender-identity values that run beneath microaggressions and that give them power to subtly define reality for targeted subjects. The occurrence of a microaggressive statement may be used to illustrate the subtle ways oppressive ideologies and theologies are communicated through often-unintentional verbal expression in classroom and pulpit. This serves the dual purpose of bringing latent, unexamined theologies into the foreground for sustained critical conversation and of depleting the microaggressive act of its most insidious power over racial, gender, or LGBTQ minority students in the classroom—namely, *attributional ambiguity.*

Beyond a covenant to support one another in the careful attention to language, teachers of preaching and religious education may incorporate a field into sermon or lesson evaluation forms for the "presence of potential microaggressions." This evaluative tool may be twofold, offering evaluators and the student preacher an opportunity to assess the potential presence of microaggressive speech within delivered sermons.

Questions for the evaluator's report might include these:

- What was the potential microaggression? (Render verbatim if possible.)
- Was this a microinsult, a microinvalidation, or a microassault? (Circle one.)
- What is the subtle message you believe was being communicated?
- What theological belief(s) or assumption(s) did you see being conveyed in this communication?

Questions for the student's consideration might include these:

- Do you agree with the assessment of this as a microaggression? If so, were you aware of the microaggressive potential of this statement?
- Was the message communicated to this evaluator your *intended* message? If not, what did you *wish* to communicate?
- Does the theological belief or assumption thought to underlie this communication accord with your deliberative theology? That is, does it represent what you consciously believe or think about the subject?
- After considering these questions, how do you wish to address this communication?

In the evaluative process, instructors must allow for their own communications to be subject to intentional metacommunication about the microaggressive potential of speech, thus modeling an openness to address potential microaggressions when they arise in classroom communication.

Finally, critical engagement of microaggressions in the classroom attends to the inner narratives of students in ways that promote development of pastoral concern for the inner narratives of their congregants. In regular day-to-day interaction, victims of microaggressions must ask themselves three questions: "Did this microaggression really occur?" "Should I respond to this microaggression?" and "How should I respond to this microaggression?"[15] In either the seminary or the church classroom, these questions should be programmatic for all students and co-learners rather than an isolated mental exercise reserved for those students who may at any point become targets of in-class microaggressions. Instructors and students must cultivate a corporate understanding that microaggressions should be responded to in the liminal space of the classroom and that constructive models of response should be modeled *to* students and developed further *by* students prior to any student's ever having to internally deliberate whether or how to respond when a micro-aggression occurs.

In this way, both seminary classrooms and church education programs may equip students and participants to address the potential of microaggressions outside of the classroom. Churches and seminaries may become places of strengthening and healing for students who develop new tools and abilities to address microaggressions in their everyday lives. Nadal offers several tools that may be practiced in classroom spaces. For example, he suggests paraphrasing back to the speaker what the speaker has just said immediately after the speaker finishes speaking. This paraphrasing can be done by a classroom facilitator or fellow student, and it has the effect of clarifying the content, perspective, and meaning in the immediate aftermath of a potentially microaggressive communication. The one paraphrasing may then ask the original speaker whether or not the paraphrase accurately captures what the speaker intended to communicate.[16] The answer may then open up dialogical space to examine the gap that exists between what one intends to say and the subtle, unintentional messages that listeners hear.

Nadal reminds us that, as much as microaggressions may be painful to hear and may raise feelings of anger in teachers and fellow students alike, it is vital that classroom conversations about microaggressions remain nonpunitive.[17] One way of engaging in nonpunitive confrontations is to label the communication one has experienced as "potentially microaggressive," rather than "racist" or "homophobic."[18] One may go on to explain what one heard in the communication, perhaps even using the paraphrasing exercise above. The point of these conversations should never be to punish or shame speakers. Rather, communicating openly about the presence and experience of microaggressions in classroom spaces holds the potential to confront microaggressions in constructive ways that ultimately make classrooms in churches and educational institutions places where concern for the physical, psychological, and spiritual well-being of students is taken into greater account.

As Sue argues, "Reducing ambiguity and uncertainty and making the invisible visible would do much to lower the stress levels among marginalized groups . . . giving oppressed groups the language and concepts to speak about their experiences, to be able to name the offenses, to be liberated, and to feel empowered by the understanding of their experiences."[19] Taking seriously the presence of microaggressions and their potential to harm in our seminary classrooms, religious education programs, and pulpits means attending to the subtleties of our verbal communications. This skill communicates pastoral concern for both students and their parishioners, modeling language to speak about experiences of microaggressive violence that have previously gone unnamed. A church or seminary expressing this linguistic pastoral concern is most certainly a gift in the life of its parishioners and students.

Chapter 7

Microaggressions in Music, Space, and Prayer

Worship and Spirituality

Baby, You Were Born This Way

*I*t was a rare Sunday when a certain opening and affirming church abandoned the lectionary, which is the three-year rotation of Scripture lessons used by most mainline churches, and dedicated its entire worship service to celebrating Pride. (The day before, the pastors had gathered with over fifty congregants to march in their city's LGBTQ Pride parade.) The staff had spent a lot of time carefully, prayerfully, and intentionally planning worship. The worship planning staff was composed of two pastors—a lesbian woman and a gay man—a music minister who was also a gay man, and the chair of the worship committee, a straight woman who considered herself an ally.

Since the popular artist Lady Gaga had recently released her chart-topping hit "Born This Way," the staff had wanted worship to make a playful nod at her song by reminding LGBTQ people that they are made in the image of God, beloved, and worthwhile. Worship began by subverting the traditional Old One Hundredth hymn, with voices rising in four-part harmony:

> Between the lesbian, gay, and straight,
> no longer we'll be bound by hate.

Tears flowed. Queer folk felt redeemed. It was a holy moment, an extraordinary morning when the sacred broke through and entered the worship service. A family of two fathers and two children read the call to worship as the congregation responded, "Made in the image of God, we were born beautiful."

The gay male pastor led the children's sermon by playing a clip of Lady Gaga's song. Everyone giggled and applauded as the children talked about how it's okay to be different because "it's how God made you!" The lesbian pastor preached on Ephesians 2:10, reminding the gays and lesbians in the congregation that they are God's workmanship—in Greek, God's *poema*. It's where we derive our English word for poem. "God wrote a magnificent poem and titled it with your name. God's fingerprints are all over you," she told her congregation. Their lesbian preacher proclaimed these words, her queer body behind the pulpit, the place typically reserved for straight men.

Following worship, congregants thanked the staff for the prophetic service. "This is what Jesus means when he told us to care for the least among us. The gays: we're the least among us in our society," they said. The staff agreed, proud of the work they were doing, hugging the children of gay and lesbian parents, patting the backs of straight allies who had marched with them the day prior. This community needed to feel pride. They needed to be reminded that they are fearfully and wonderfully made. They needed affirmation and welcome.

Days later, a congregant asked to meet with one of the pastors to discuss the transgender support group he leads. The pastor felt even more pride. "Aren't we a wonderful church," she thought, "marching in the Pride parade, queering hymns, and hosting a transgender support group?" It's the way church should be.

After discussing some details regarding the support group, the congregant broached the topic of the Pride worship service. The pastor prepared herself for accolades, ready to celebrate how fabulous and queer and holy the church was. Instead, the transgender congregant told her, "It's great to tell gays, lesbians, and bisexuals that they're made in the image of God and they're God's beautiful poem. I can totally see how affirming that is. But the T in LGBTQ was missing in worship on Sunday. The T is always missing, always invisible, always the least." The pastor felt ashamed, disappointed, and asked him to say more. With tears in his eyes, he blurted out, "God made a big mistake on me. God created me in a female body, and my parents wrapped me in a pink blanket and dressed me in pink dresses. All the while, I'm a man. I'm a man. Doesn't God see that?"

In the worship staff's eager attempt to queer worship in the direction of justice and inclusion, they had planned the service in such a way that the voices and bodies and realities of their transgender congregants were ignored. Like many gays and lesbians, they'd turned Scripture on its head, subverting portions of the Bible otherwise used to damn gays to hell. By utilizing narratives from creation, they ignored how hurtful and exclusive such theologies can be to individuals struggling with their gendered identity. It took a brave transgender man to teach his gay and lesbian worship staff what it means to care about the least among us.

The pastor listened carefully to her congregant's words. She felt deep remorse and a strange tension. On the one hand, so many gay and lesbian congregants left worship feeling affirmed and loved, some for the first time ever. The pastor wanted to honor and celebrate this. At the same time, however, it was clear that worship had also marginalized the transgender persons in the congregation. The pastor apologized and thanked her congregant for having the courage to talk with her. She asked his permission to talk with the worship staff about it. After he agreed, the pastor called a special meeting with the worship staff to discuss what had happened.

At first, the music minister thought the transgender congregant was making a big deal out of nothing. "People were in tears. Good tears. Tears of finally being affirmed in church. That should be celebrated. Gay people *are* made that way, and God loves them, and our worship reflected that!" It was difficult to hear a critique of such a moving and meaningful service. After reflecting, sharing, and praying together, though, the staff realized that while worship had been tremendously affirming for many, it had been disenfranchising to others. They realized that they had acted out of their own cisgender privilege by never imagining how worship would impact their transgender congregants. They decided to craft a service of affirmation and reconciliation as a response. One of the pastors called the transgender congregant who initiated the conversation to ask for his input. He suggested talking with the entire transgender support group.

That week, the staff was invited as guests to a meeting of the transgender support group, and together they crafted a service of affirmation and reconciliation. The following Sunday, the worship staff stood together during the period of announcements and spoke about how many people had been moved by worship the previous Sunday, but that worship had also greatly hurt others. They invited everyone to return that evening for a service of affirmation and reconciliation. Some people couldn't understand what was problematic and refused to come. Others didn't get it but wanted to be understanding, and so they attended. Still others attended because they were, indeed, hurt and in need of affirmation and reconciliation.

The service was informal, touching, and filled with heartfelt moments of forgiveness. A few transgender congregants shared their stories. The entire worship staff apologized for overlooking the needs of people vital to their community. As a result, the transgender members of the congregation felt much safer in worship.

Intersectional Identities, Intersectional Spiritualities

A progressive interdenominational seminary in a large urban metropolis selects a theme each year for its annual student-faculty-staff retreat. The theme for this year was "Celebrating Spiritualities." A small group of students was charged with planning the retreat under the guidance of the professor of spirituality. Since the demographics of the students, faculty, and staff are remarkably diverse, the planning group wanted to provide opportunities for everyone to draw on elements of their own spiritual heritage. Accordingly, the schedule provided two opportunities—one on Saturday and one on Sunday—for people to attend one of the following spirituality groups: women's spirituality, African American spirituality, Latino/a spirituality, LGBTQ spirituality, Asian spirituality, or men's spirituality. Each group had a well-trained leader who represented the particular spiritual heritage being discussed. The planning committee studied the seminary's demographics carefully to ensure that everyone was represented and no one would feel excluded.

When the time came on Saturday for everyone to select a spiritual heritage group, students, faculty, and staff divided into small groups and met in separate rooms. About eighteen people gathered in the women's spirituality group and began sharing some of their experiences. When the time came for Teresa to share, she was visibly frustrated and held back angry tears. "I'm really struggling with what to say here," she said quietly.

"Speak from your heart," the group leader, Amy, encouraged. "It's okay. We're all women here. We understand how much of a struggle it can be."

"That's exactly what's so hard," Teresa said, her voice rising with anger. "You *don't* understand. Like you, I am a woman. But I'm also Asian. Why should I have to choose between women's spirituality and Asian spirituality? And in case you've forgotten, I'm also a lesbian. How am I supposed to decide which part of me needs the most spirituality? The woman part? The Asian part? The lesbian part? It's not like I can take off some of these parts of myself! They're all a part of who I am."

Jamie, a white lesbian, spoke up, "I'm really glad you brought this up, Teresa. I was feeling the same way as a lesbian. Do I choose women's spirituality or LGBTQ spirituality?" An African American woman named Bianca responded, "I feel the same way. Being black is really important to my identity, but so is being a woman. Why should I have to choose?"

Amy didn't know what to do. Though she was trained to lead the group on women's spirituality, she wasn't trained to respond to these issues. "I appreciate all of you sharing your concerns, but let's not derail the conversation any further. Let's move on by discussing the history of women's spirituality." An awkward lecture with brief moments of forced discussion followed for the next forty-five minutes. Teresa, Jamie, and Bianca left feeling angry, invalidated, and as though their intersectional identities didn't really matter to the group leader or to their seminary. "Why would they plan a retreat like this?" the three women asked one another after the session ended.

Amy left the session feeling horrible. She had no idea how to handle the situation and simply chose to follow the rubric provided for her. Amy immediately found the professor and shared what had happened. The professor felt foolish for not anticipating such a concern and asked Amy to gather together the entire planning committee immediately. After Amy shared with the committee what had happened with her group, another member responded by sharing that a gay Latino faculty member had shared a similar concern in the LGBTQ spirituality group.

The professor and the members of the student committee felt incredibly embarrassed that they had overlooked such an important part of their community and of spirituality. "How can someone feel spiritually fulfilled if they have to separate parts of themselves into silos, as though one or two parts of their identity are more important than the others?" one student asked. "How can we fix this?" asked another. The members agreed that they could not repair the damage that had already been done, but they could take responsibility for their actions, apologize, and propose a new way of moving forward. They decided to reorganize the rest of the retreat beginning with the big group spirituality event planned for that evening. In its place, they decided to hold an open forum where people could share their experiences of intersectionality and exclusion. Punctuating each moment of sharing, everyone would engage in silent and guided prayer.

Before beginning the evening session, the members of the planning committee stood together and apologized to everyone gathered. "We are very sorry that the way we divided spirituality groups forced some in our community to feel excluded, divided, or marginalized," the professor told the group. "As a professor in such a beautifully diverse community, I should have known better. I should have thought about what these groupings would mean to each and every one of our students, faculty, and staff. Instead, I guided our students in organizing groupings that suit my own starting point. This decision came without acknowledging my own privileges, and I am truly sorry. We are so grateful that some of our students, faculty, and staff expressed concern. Together, we want to make changes to the schedule so that none of you have to leave a part of yourselves on the shelf. Every part of you is a part of your spirituality, and every part of you is important at our seminary. I would never want our programming to forsake this vital truth."

Teresa, Jamie, Bianca, and others who had voiced similar concerns felt that the apology was sincere, though they were still hurt that it had occurred in the first place. The evening spirituality event proved meaningful and healing for many. Together, the students, faculty, and staff determined that forcing people to choose one element of their "heritage" over others was not life giving or fair. They also agreed on a new schedule for Sunday that provided different meeting times for each of the smaller spirituality groups so that individuals with intersectional identities would not have to forsake any of their identities by choosing one grouping over another. Some individuals with intersectional identities chose to attend only one session, while others attended two or three. All were grateful that they did not have to silo any part of their spiritual heritage.

Amy also had individual conversations with Teresa, Jamie, and Bianca in which she apologized for how she had handled their group meeting. "I should have listened better and taken this as an opportunity for all of us to talk about and learn about intersectionality," she told them. Amy also decided to write a letter to the eighteen women who attended her session and apologize. Moving forward, Amy, the professor, and the rest of the planning committee made it a point to learn more about intersectionality. And students, faculty, and staff with intersectional identities felt more affirmed following the retreat with the knowledge that their identities were not going to be forced apart any longer at their seminary.

Constructive Tools for Addressing Microaggressions in Worship

The transgender congregant in this chapter's opening vignette offers a prime example of how worship has the potential to microaggressively assault individuals longing for meaningful connections with the Divine through corporate worship. At the same time, however, the response of the pastors and worship planning team illustrates that recognizing microaggressive actions, taking responsibility for such actions, apologizing, and working to reconcile with those hurt is possible. In this section, we discuss how to address microaggressions in worship by understanding the impact of our language, music, art, and architecture. We also briefly address how two key components of Christian worship can function subversively as acts of resistance for those dealing with microaggressions: Communion and baptism.

Since chapter 6 is dedicated to preaching, we will not concentrate on this element of the spoken word here. Instead, the role of nonmicroaggressive speech is primary in constructing liturgical language that is affirming and inclusive. As addressed in chapter 4, gender-inclusive language is an important part of creating worship that is expansive. Liturgical language operates on six levels, beginning with the most exclusive and progressing toward more and more diversity: (1) exclusive language, (2) inclusive language for humanity, (3) neutral inclusive language for God, (4) particular inclusive language, (5) queer language, and (6) nonmicroaggressive expansive language.

Most churches, seminaries, and denominations still use exclusive language for humanity, adhering to translations of Scripture—such as the KJV, the NIV, and the ASV—that use masculine nouns and pronouns when referring to groups of men, women, and children. Employing such language when reading Scripture, praying, or reciting litanies functions exclusively and is sexist.

Most progressive churches, seminaries, and denominations acknowledge the sexism of exclusive language for humanity by highlighting the patriarchal context in which Scripture was written. Such communities would proclaim "peace to all people," for example, rather than saying "peace to all men." Many of these same communities acknowledge that Scripture and other liturgical language—prayers, litanies, and responsive readings—also include harmful binaries related to light and darkness that are microaggressively racist in nature. For example, darkness and shadows are equated with life before Christ, while Christ is associated with light. Similarly, sin is often described as black, while purity is described as white. Given the historical claims that persons of color do not have souls, are not worth saving, or do not have the capacity to become Christian, such language harkens back to these incredibly racist histories embedded in the church and wider society. Consequently, using such language today is also racist in nature.

Once a community uses inclusive language for humanity, the third step on the way toward expansive language is evoking gender-neutral language for God. We contend that the vast majority of religious communities claiming to value diversity and inclusion stop at this particular form of liturgical language. In gender-neutral inclusive language, God is neither *he* nor *she;* Scripture readings, prayers, litanies, and responsive readings that reference God do not use pronouns at all. As discussed in chapter 4, such replacements function as a step along the way toward inclusion. But this step is not enough. When most individuals hear "God," they automatically perceive in their mind a male because God is understood as male in most religious traditions and in the wider society. Accordingly, our language must be more particular in order to become more expansive. The fourth step, as also discussed in chapter 4, involves particular inclusive language.[1]

The fifth step in moving toward expansive liturgical language is using language that is queer. Queering our liturgical language steps beyond acknowledging only gender and also includes sexuality. A primary function of queer studies is to dismantle binary categories of sex and gender. With forced binaries inevitably come hierarchies in which one binary is elevated at the expense of the other. For example, in most liturgical language, man is valued over woman, straight is valued over gay, father is valued over mother, and white is valued over black. Language that is queer seeks to dismantle these binaries as false constructions created by society. In deconstructing these oppressive binaries, we can reconstruct language that is inclusive. For example, rather than addressing God as "Father" or even "Mother" in a prayer, the liturgist may call God "Beloved" or "Lover." Rather than constantly evoking gender binaries by calling the congregation "brothers and sisters" or "ladies and gentlemen," liturgists can call everyone "family," "beloved community," or "children of God." As exemplified in the vignette of the Pride worship service, many open and affirming communities work hard to queer their language in ways that celebrate the diversity of humankind. As the transgender congregant pointed out, however, queer worship planners are not exempt from microaggressive speech. For this reason, a sixth and final step is needed for all liturgical language to be expansive and inclusive of everyone.

This final step is liturgical language that is nonmicroaggressive. When crafting prayers, liturgies, and other words spoken during worship, it is imperative that liturgists consider how their words may impact the "least among us." During Holy Week, for example, it is important to consider the racist ramifications of using darkness as a symbol for the time when Jesus died. How might such language impact persons of color who have been demonized, oppressed, or marginalized because of the darkness of their skin? How might we deepen and broaden our language to be more expansive rather than adhering to the traditionally racist binaries that equate darkness with sin, death, and badness and that equate lightness with life, newness, and goodness? Similarly, during the season of Advent, liturgists should consider what it would feel like for LGBTQ persons—who are repeatedly told by myriad churches and by the wider society that being queer is sinful and needs to be corrected—to hear that the crooked pathways should be made "straight." Might we shift our language so that pathways become direct or plumb?

Since one of the central messages Jesus preached was to take care of the least among us, it is incumbent on us to consider the least when crafting our liturgical language for worship. We must question the language of the prayer books or the liturgies provided by denominational bodies. If the language is racist, sexist, heterosexist, or transphobic, we must change it. When writing our own liturgies and prayers, we should always pause to ask, "How might these words be heard by persons of color, women, and LGBTQs?" If the language risks harming, marginalizing, or invalidating anyone, we do not need to use it.

Not only must our liturgical language resist microaggressions, but so too must our music. As so-called worship wars abound and some congregations even split over styles of worship, it is important to acknowledge the complexity of conversations about music. Resisting microaggressions that assault the souls of worshipers, however, is not about style or preference. It is not about organs competing with guitars or praise songs battling with hymns. Instead, nonmicroaggressive music, like nonmicroaggressive language, considers how music will impact the least among us.

Congregations, denominations, and seminaries that only sing or play music composed by straight, white men are engaging in racist, sexist, and heteronormative microaggressive behaviors. This can be difficult to hear, particularly when specific hymns, songs, or musical compositions deeply resonate and touch an individual or community's spirit. Hear us clearly: Listening to Mozart or singing hymns composed by Wesley is not inherently racist, sexist, or heterosexist. The problem is if the community *only* or *mostly* sings and listens to such music. Though often not as popular or as well-known, there are a robust number of hymns, spirituals, and praise songs composed by persons of color, women, and LGBTQs. We can expand our musical knowledge by learning about such music, and then we can introduce it to our faith community. When doing so, we can teach the community about the stories and histories that accompany the music.

Teaching communities about the music, in addition to singing the music, is vital when utilizing global music. Songs of praise stem from every inch of the globe, and our communities limit their worship and theology if they only sing songs written and composed by white male composers in English. By learning the histories and stories behind particular songs and teaching them to churches, liturgists and music ministers remind congregations that our faith expands beyond our communities, languages, and traditions. When singing in a different language, it is a good idea to consult someone fluent in that language in order to avoid pronouncing words incorrectly. Worship can be an opportunity to teach the church about this process of learning to sing the words of another culture.

In planning worship, invite a diverse array of people to join the process so that a variety of backgrounds and perspectives may be present. This can also help avoid tokenizing oppressed persons and communities. For example, it is important to include music composed by African Americans every Sunday and not simply during Black History Month or on Martin Luther King Jr. Sunday. Singing songs composed by women is needed every time the community gathers for worship and not only during Women's History Month or on Mother's Day. Singing global music is vital each week and not merely on

World Communion Sunday. If we truly want to be the beloved community where every person is valued, included, and affirmed, our music must reflect that.

In addition to nonmicroaggressive language and music, the use of art and architecture is also part of being an inclusive and expansive community. If iconography, stained glass, bulletin covers, and other art and images depicted in worship portray a white Jesus, or only white and male saints and biblical figures, such artwork has microaggressive potential to assault the souls of persons of color and women. There are powerful images of the crucified Christ, for example, that portray Christ as a black man amid the shadows of a lynching tree, a raped woman stripped naked with legs spread on the horizontal crossbar of the cross, or a gay man with the word *faggot* superimposed over *King of the Jews*. Such art not only evokes diversity and represents the multiplicity of humankind, but it also points us toward the ways countless oppressed persons are crucified throughout history and in contemporary society. In the same ways that our liturgical language and music must consider the least among us, so too must our art and architecture.

Architecture is often most difficult to change because it is so permanent and expensive. If clergy are seated on a raised platform with the congregation beneath them on pews facing forward in rows, what does this communicate about who and what is most valuable in worship? This communication deepens when every person seated on the platform is white, or male, or straight. Though we have not addressed issues of ability in this book, microaggressions can also assault the souls of persons who are differently abled. If someone in a wheelchair cannot ascend the platform to speak at the podium or sing in the choir, the church's architecture communicates a theology that says, "Only normatively abled bodies are valued here. If you cannot ascend the platform, you are not as worthy as those who can." While deconstructing an entire sanctuary may prove too costly, there are ways to avoid such microaggressions in architecture. Moving the platform furniture to the same level as the rest of the congregation is one easy step a community can take to be more inclusive. Building a ramp, ensuring that there is a diversity of humanity seated on the platform, or replacing pews with movable chairs that can be arranged in a semicircle are also more inclusive options.

In addition to the visual art and architecture seen on a regular basis in worship, there are also visual components of liturgy that should be questioned. For example, many Catholic and mainline Protestant churches participate in Tenebrae worship on Maundy Thursday or Good Friday. Tenebrae is a service of shadows. Traditionally, worship begins with many lit candles, with the Christ candle largest and centered. As different passages from the passion narratives are read and sung, candles are extinguished. Simultaneously, black cloth is used to cloak elements of "life and light" in the sanctuary. Greenery, the baptismal font, the extinguished candles, the pulpit, and even the cross are covered in black cloth. At the end of worship, when the biblical text speaks of Jesus' death, the Christ candle is extinguished and covered with a black cloth. Worshipers often leave the space in silence and darkness. For many, Tenebrae is a necessary step on the way toward resurrection on Easter. In these ways, it is a tremendously moving worship service that evokes the power of death, visually and tangibly reminding worshipers of Jesus' crucifixion. These are things that are important to the Christian tradition. In and of itself, Tenebrae is an evocative reminder.

Consider, however, some of the microaggressively racist implications embedded in such worship when partnered with microaggressively racist liturgical language and music. If a church does not sing or play any music composed by persons of color, if the language of darkness and blackness is equated with sin and death, if all the images of Jesus and saints are white, how might a person of color feel when attending the Tenebrae service? How might that same person feel on returning on Easter Sunday when all the black cloths—the representations of death—are removed and the cross, the altar, and the vestments are all cloaked in white? To some, this may seem like a far reach. Tenebrae is a pivotal part of liturgical Christian worship traditions. But if you examine such worship through the lens of an anthropologist outside of the Christian tradition, what you observe is worship that one day is somberly focused on death and is completely black and worship that another day is celebratory, full of life, and completely white. In these ways, elements of a traditional Tenebrae worship service are microaggressively racist and in need of changing. This does not necessarily mean that Tenebrae must be forsaken or that we must rush to resurrection without experiencing crucifixion. Acknowledging the complexity of equating darkness with death and sin within the confines of worship is one nonmicroaggressive action that has powerful potential. Replacing black cloths with cloths that are deep purple may be another.

Whether it is liturgical language, music, art, architecture, or the visual components often overlooked in liturgy, worship has the power to affirm or exclude. As evidenced by the vignette that opened this chapter, even the most thoughtful and prayerful worship runs the risk of being microaggressive if worship planners do not acknowledge the privileges they bring to the planning process and consider how worship may impact the least among us.

In addition to worship leaders utilizing the tools we have addressed regarding liturgical language, music, art, and architecture, two sacraments—or ordinances, depending on one's tradition—are also important to provide worshipers with opportunities to cope with microaggressions. These include Communion and baptism. Fumitaka Matsuoka and M. Shawn Copeland contend that Communion may be a symbolic resource for addressing the harm performed by microaggressions. Matsuoka claims, "Our challenge is not merely to struggle against an unjust society that stifles dignity. The challenge is to recover speech that permits communion with one another, to break bread together, a communion for which people so deeply yearn and we Christians confess to be our deeply held value."[2] In these ways, Communion becomes a healing act, functioning like elements of spirituality that we will soon discuss. In a similar manner, Copeland evokes the need for knowledge of microaggressions at Communion:

> If my sister or brother is not at the table, we are not the flesh of Christ. If my sister's mark of sexuality must be obscured, if my brother's mark of race must be disguised, if my sister's mark of culture must be repressed, then we are not the flesh of Christ. For, it is through and in Christ's own flesh that the "other" is my sister, is my brother; indeed, the "other" is me.[3]

Recognizing that the body of Christ is not only what we break and ingest in the act of Communion, but that all bodies are part of the body of Christ, is powerful. Naming and celebrating that the body of Christ is made up a multiplicity of colors, races, ethnicities, nationalities, genders, gender identities, and sexualities is a constructive act that subverts and reimagines Communion as an act of resistance to the microaggressive behaviors of wider society.

So engaging in Communion becomes a way of coping with microaggressions in addition to providing an inclusive and diverse space. Baptism too has the possibility of celebrating this diversity and inclusion. Along these lines, Elizabeth Stuart believes that "what we receive in baptism is not an identity negotiated in conversation with our communities or culture such as our sexual and gender identities are."[4] Stuart elaborates, claiming that our baptized identity points toward a space of eschatological erasure where we are fully united in Christ:

> The baptized belong to another world. To be baptized is to be caught up in a kingdom that does not yet fully exist, that is in the process of becoming; it is to be caught up in the redemption of this world. It is not that the baptized are called to live beyond culture, but that they are called to transform culture by living in it in such a way as to testify to the other world being born within it.[5]

As Stuart reminds us, baptism in particular (and worship more broadly) offers us the possibility, privilege, and responsibility of creating a space where unity in Christ is celebrated amid our diversity and difference. Worship is a place where we can transform our wider society to be a place of radical inclusion and hospitality.

Constructive Tools for Addressing Microaggressions in Spirituality

As evidenced throughout much of this book, very little research exists that discusses the role of microaggressions in faith communities and religious institutions. On the topics of preaching, religious education, or worship, few if any publications can be found that include microaggressions. Such is also true when it comes to microaggressions and spirituality. With the exception of a dissertation by Lloyd Sheldon Johnson, we have been unable to find any work on spirituality that includes microaggressions.

At the University of Massachusetts Boston, Johnson wrote an insightful dissertation on spirituality as a resource for black men in responding to racial microaggressions while attending community college.[6] Throughout his research, Johnson discovered that spirituality provided black males who attended community college with compassion, forgiveness, inner strength, and empathy when they encountered racial microaggressions. This is in line with myriad medical studies that also have emphasized the importance of spiritual practices—such as prayer or meditation—in dealing with stress.[7] We have seen throughout this book that microaggressions are a tremendous cause of stress, so one could readily deduce that spiritual practices are one important way of dealing with microaggressions. Such practices provide victims of microaggressions the capacity to address the negative ways discrimination has impacted their health physically, emotionally, and spiritually. In these ways, Johnson's findings are reflective of how the broader medical field advocates for spiritual practices as a way to cope with stress.

If a woman experiences gender-based microaggressions in her workplace, praying with her faith community may provide the balm needed for coping. When a person of color encounters racial microaggressions in public settings, meditation may offer helpful ways of coping and of easing stress. After an LGBTQ person experiences microaggressions at school, that person may be put at ease by attending an embodied spirituality group at church. These are all real possibilities for oppressed persons grappling with microaggressive behaviors. As Johnson contends, it is the church's responsibility to provide spiritual support for the downtrodden. Applying his work directly to black males, Johnson claims, "Church leaders function as advocates for liberation and freedom for Blacks. . . . [Historically] Churches were the steppingstones to education and liberation, for they provided a moral and ethical foundation for their members."[8] Similarly, churches—and church leaders—have a moral obligation to provide a safe haven, a place of spiritual nourishment for those who are oppressed and marginalized. As we have seen, however, the church does not always act like a place of liberation and freedom.

We affirm Johnson and other educators and medical professionals who encourage spiritual practices as a way of coping with stress. This is good and important and true. What is problematic is when the spiritual communities who are supposed to provide liberation and freedom instead offer more microaggressive behaviors that only deepen the stress and pain that marginalized persons are experiencing. In the case of Teresa, we witnessed how representatives of a progressive seminary assaulted the soul of a person whose gender, race, and sexuality were marginalized by her own spiritual community. If Teresa had remained silent, kept her pain to herself, and participated in all the spiritual exercises planned for the seminary's spiritual retreat, it is doubtful that those practices would have provided a balm for grappling with the microaggressions she experienced. It is even possible that engaging in those practices would have furthered her sense of invalidation and hurt because she would have continued to silo her intersectional identities by participating only in the women's spirituality group and neglecting the lesbian and Asian parts of her identity.

There is hope in the way the retreat leaders responded, however. After recognizing that the format of the retreat was oppressive, marginalizing, and microaggressive, the professor and the student leadership team took the necessary steps to apologize, listen to Teresa's experience, and reorganize the retreat in a way that valued everyone. Their response was reflective of what Kathleen Talvacchia calls the "spiritual pedagogy of multiculturalism."[9] While she never explicitly engages the language of microaggressions, Talvacchia provides useful methods for engaging diversity, difference, and multiculturalism as a spiritual practice. Placing a primary emphasis on listening to those who are marginalized, Talvacchia claims that listening leads to understanding and that understanding leads to seeing clearly and acting differently. Listening, understanding, seeing clearly, and acting differently then become spiritual practices for leaders engaged in multicultural learning and spirituality.

Accordingly, religious leaders who wish to combat microaggressions must first listen to the needs of the marginalized. They must not assume knowledge of what an individual or community needs spiritually. And while spiritual practices can serve as useful coping mechanisms for those experiencing microaggressions in their daily lives, if the spiritual practices stem from a faith community perpetrating those same microaggressions, those practices will likely be more harmful than helpful. If faith leaders engage in the imperative spiritual practice of listening, they may learn to understand, see clearly, and act in ways that will provide a balm for those experiencing microaggressions in their church, denomination, or seminary.

Chapter 8

Microaggressions in Pastoral Relationships

Care and Counseling

Confronting Transgender Microaggressions in the ER

*M*aria is a chaplain in a small community hospital in a suburban area of the U.S. South. One morning while making her rounds in the hospital's emergency department, she noticed a few nurses standing outside of a curtained-off examination room looking over a chart while whispering and giggling. As Maria walked toward the nurses, they put away the chart and dispersed. Maria heard gentle sobbing behind the curtain and decided to check on the patient to see if she could be of comfort.

When Maria pulled back the curtain, the patient looked up at her, squinting away tears. "Knock, knock. I'm Maria, the chaplain here. May I come in for a moment?"

"I suppose so," the patient answered hesitantly. Maria pulled the curtain closed behind her and approached the patient's bedside.

"I was just making my way through the emergency department this morning and wanted to see if there was anything I could do to help make you more comfortable while you are here," Maria said.

"I don't think you can make me more comfortable," the patient answered. "This is one of the most uncomfortable experiences of my life."

"I'm so sorry to hear that," Maria replied. "Are you in a lot of physical pain?"

"Not really," the patient replied. "It's mostly emotional pain at this point. The physical pain is starting to subside."

"Would you like to tell me about it?" Maria asked.

"Well, I came in to the ER very early this morning because I've been so nauseated and have had such terrible stomach pain that I couldn't even get to sleep last night. It's the worst stomachache of my life, so I just thought it would be best to get it checked out. When I came in, the nurse who brought

131

me back said, 'Good morning, sir. How can I help you?' Well, I'm used to that, especially when I haven't had time to put on any makeup. And I was just wearing this old sweat suit. So I told the nurse at the triage desk that I am a woman, and I quietly let her know that I am transgender, just in case my hormone replacement therapy and previous surgery was medically relevant. She looked at me like I had just told her I was from Mars or something."

"Oh no, that sounds like a very painful experience," Maria affirmed. "I'm so sorry."

"Well it's only gotten worse. The nurses and doctors who've come in to treat me continue to call me 'sir,' even *after* I correct them. And nurses have been gathering outside of this curtain all morning, looking over my chart and giggling and whispering about me. Even after they determined my pain was just a case of food poisoning, my nurse keeps asking me about my transition surgery and all kinds of questions that are invasive and inappropriate. This is just not the kind of treatment that I expect from a medical establishment!"

Maria remembered one of her classmates and best friends in seminary, Mark, who was transgender and who began making a female-to-male transition during their second year. Maria remembered the long conversations they had when they were supposed to be studying church history together. Mark shared with her stories of how some family members and long-time friends failed to understand what this transition meant in his life, and he expressed his gratitude that his seminary community understood and embraced him so warmly. Mark always gently corrected Maria when she would accidently refer to him with female pronouns or by his previous name. Maria was grateful to be at a seminary that fostered an atmosphere of respect and affirmation where she could learn from and alongside transgender classmates. Now she wondered how she could be most helpful to this patient.

"I am so sorry you've experienced such an inhospitable environment here—Helen, isn't it?" Maria had seen the patient's name on her chart and thought it would feel affirming to the patient to be called by her chosen, female name. "It sounds like it would feel quite invalidating to have something so fundamental to your sense of identity disrespected, questioned, and placed under scrutiny in a setting where you expected to experience compassion and care."

"Yes, that's exactly right! Invalidated! That is a perfect way to describe how I've felt these past few hours. It has been so painful. Thank you for understanding, Reverend," Helen replied with tears in her eyes. "I just wish there was some way others in my shoes wouldn't have to go through this same kind of experience. It is so common for transgender people I know when they have to come to the hospital or go to a new doctor."

Maria felt the same desire as she reflected on Helen's experience and wondered to herself whether her seminary friend, Mark, ever had similar experiences.

"I wonder if you might find it helpful for me to introduce you to someone we have at the hospital called a patient advocate. Patient advocates consider matters of patient rights when it comes to things like privacy and confidentiality. They also help to raise awareness among other staff members of the hospital about issues that pertain to quality patient care. I know one of the advocates covering the emergency department. She is very empathic, and I think she would appreciate hearing about your experience this morning."

"That would be wonderful," Helen replied. "Anything that might help make things better for trans people here in the future. Thank you so much for listening and understanding."

Maria introduced Helen to the patient advocate and checked back in with Helen before she was discharged. After seeing Helen off, Maria returned to the Office of Spiritual Care, wondering how her role as a chaplain extends beyond individual care for patients to the cultivation of an ethic of care in the midst of oppressive circumstances within the institution. Maria decided to talk with the director of spiritual care about arranging educational opportunities about transgender concerns for the staff chaplains and spiritual care volunteers. She also set up an appointment the following week with the director of nursing education to share her experience with Helen and to offer her assistance in setting up a lunch-and-learn session on transgender patient care for interested nurses. Maria knows that Helen's experience is all too common at hospitals across the country, but she hopes that her caregiving and advocacy will make a difference for patients at her institution.

Addressing Racial Tokenism in the Congregation

Anthony and Cheryl are an African American couple in their early forties who have attended St. John's Church consistently for over a year. St. John's is a midsize parish in the suburbs of a large city in the Midwest. They began attending St. John's over a year ago because it is the parish closest to their home within their denominational tradition. They enjoy the church's music and social justice ministries.

In the past several months, Anthony and Cheryl have noticed how many committees they have been asked to join. They recognize that to this predominantly white congregation dedicated to social justice concerns, their presence and perspective as African Americans is highly valued. Cheryl, who attended a small Christian liberal arts college with a student body that was 95 percent white, is quite used to this dynamic. Anthony, on the other hand, attended a historically black university and finds the dynamic a bit amusing. Given that they often don't possess any particular interest or expertise in the areas of committee work they are invited to join, at times they feel like the token racial minority in these groups. But they often just joke with one another about doing their "diversity duty" at church—being the sole persons of color in most classes, activities, and committee meetings.

Lately, however, several conversations have struck them as particularly troubling. Some of the women in Cheryl's book group were discussing race relations in the United States. A few of the women boldly claimed that they were simply color-blind when it came to race. One of them turned to Cheryl and said, "Like Cheryl, here. When she came to St. John's, I didn't see a *black* woman. I just saw a smart, attractive, accomplished woman. Isn't that how you would want to be seen, Cheryl? I think we need *more* racial minorities like you in our church!"

Cheryl didn't quite know what to say. She felt demeaned that her racial identity was something that this fellow congregant needed to ignore in order to be in community with her. "And what did she mean by 'more racial minorities like you'?" she thought. "Does my education, or economic class, or professional vocation somehow whitewash my racial identity in her mind?" But Cheryl also knew that the woman's heart was in the right place, as evidenced by her commitment to the racial justice initiatives of the congregation. Cheryl felt embarrassed and put on the spot and a little angry, so she just nodded and politely added, "Well, my race is an important part of who I am." The conversation moved on without any acknowledgment of the problematic nature of the "color-blind" statement.

A few weeks later, Pastor Stanley, the senior minister of the congregation, invited Anthony and Cheryl to coffee. They had a wide-ranging, informal conversation, but when Pastor Stanley asked Anthony and Cheryl how they had experienced being two of the only African American members of the congregation, they looked at each other and smiled a little. "It's been fine," Anthony said. "We've felt warmly welcomed into the church and are encouraged by your sermons that address issues of racial justice in the community."

Wondering about the mutual glance and laughter, Pastor Stanley asked what that had been about. They laughed again and told the pastor about their "diversity duty" jokes, about all of their committee invitations, and about their difficulties in figuring out how to address the slightly insulting comments that people in the church had unknowingly made about race. "It's a wonderful congregation, Pastor Stanley," Anthony added. "We really do feel warmly embraced here. It's just that sometimes good white liberals don't quite know how to deal with racial differences without tokenizing or acting like they've been suddenly stricken with a case of color blindness."

Pastor Stanley had long been concerned with helping the congregation move from practices of racial tokenism toward cultivating a community shaped by an ethic of racial justice. He was both unsurprised and a bit disheartened to hear this report from Anthony and Cheryl and was concerned about their continued emotional well-being within the congregation.

"Thank you for trusting me enough to share that with me. It sounds like we have a ways to go as a congregation to really embody our commitments to racial justice in everyday practice. The color-blind nonsense is something I've been addressing for years among my white colleagues and congregants," Pastor Stanley shared. He also affirmed that he believed a denial of color is a denial of racial differences and, ultimately, a denial of the ways white people profit from racial privilege. He spoke of it as an abdication of responsibility for taking any action against the unquestioned structures of racism.[1] Anthony and Cheryl enthusiastically nodded in agreement to what Pastor Stanley shared.

"Cheryl and Anthony, I'm thinking of having some folks over to my house after the Christmas season is over to talk about the future of our congregation's racial justice commitments. I've been thinking of inviting Rev. Jack, a retired white minister from another denomination who is now a member of St. John's with a long history of racial justice work; a young adult couple you may not know, also white, who have expressed a passion for making St. John's a welcoming place for all; and Janice, a Japanese-American woman who's been a part of the congregation for two decades. Would you be interested in coming? These members are really invested in helping cultivate an ethic of racial justice in the congregation, and I know they would be very understanding of the challenges represented by your experiences."

Cheryl and Anthony were energized by the thought of helping St. John's move beyond racial tokenism toward more robust commitments of racial justice. Pastor Stanley was hopeful that the emerging conversation in this small group would lead the larger congregation to face the reality of tokenism and the perils of color-blind ideology. He also hoped that this conversation would begin to build a framework for congregants to understand and address race-based microaggressions—a concept he would introduce to the small group at their first meeting—in a variety of other contexts outside of the church walls. Stanley felt invigorated as a pastor by being able to help his parishioners with their personal, individual experience of racial microaggressions by cultivating space for them to practice their commitments to racial justice within the congregation and beyond.

Constructive Tools for Addressing Microaggressions in Care and Counseling

What does it mean to practice care in the midst of systemic subtleties of microaggressive violence against embodiments of human difference? This question is situated squarely in the midst of substantive paradigm shifts in the fields of pastoral theology, care, and counseling. This period of ferment, which has gone on for the last couple of decades, is leading practitioners of care and counseling beyond overly individualistic models of care and toward practices that account for systemic and political factors of oppression, injustice, and violence affecting the well-being of both individuals and communities.

The clinical paradigm predominant in the field for the past several decades focuses on practices of care that address the individual and draws heavily on psychological models of understanding human predicaments. While helpful in many regards in assisting pastoral caregivers to understand the complexities of human experience, the clinical paradigm has operated largely without sufficient attention to the political and social consequences of the social context on the well-being of individuals.[2] Slowly taking the clinical paradigm's place of primacy in the field over the past couple of decades, a "communal contextual" paradigm, guided by the work of figures such as John Patton and Larry Graham, has shifted the attention of caregivers beyond the individual alone to account for the ways social, cultural, and political contexts affect the lives of individuals and communities.[3] Additionally, an "intercultural paradigm" has emerged from the work of pastoral theologians such as Emmanuel Lartey that attempts to foreground for caregivers the role of cultural, racial, and religious pluralism in contexts of care while critiquing the ethically problematic privileging of Eurocentric hegemony within many practices of care.[4] These paradigms shape the point of view of pastoral theologians and caregivers, shifting the focus of care to account for individual psychological dynamics and toward a careful examination of wider sociocultural settings into which the lives of care seekers are situated. Consequently, these paradigm shifts in the field also have shifted the practices of care that emerge from these perspectives.

William Clebsch and Charles Jaekle famously named the four practical functions of pastoral care as *healing, sustaining, guiding,* and *reconciling.*[5]

Through healing, pastoral care functions to restore one to a condition of wholeness, assisting care seekers to achieve new levels of spiritual insight and well-being. Sustaining care occurs during times in which the circumstance or condition that calls for care cannot be transcended, such as cases of bereavement. Caregivers exercise the function of guidance in helping care seekers to make choices between alternative courses of action by drawing on the seekers' experiences, resources, and values. Clebsch and Jaekle see the reconciliation function operating to repair relationships between persons and between individuals and God, drawing on resources of the Christian tradition such as forgiveness. The shape of pastoral care in clinical and congregational contexts over the past several decades is indicative of the centrality of these four functions of care and their importance in the lives of care seekers. But as sociocultural contexts became foregrounded more and more within pastoral care and counseling, pastoral theologians began imagining pastoral practice beyond these four functions of care in ways important when considering care and counseling approaches to microaggressions.

Womanist pastoral theologian Carroll Watkins Ali expands these four functions of pastoral care through critical pastoral theological reflection on the themes of survival and liberation in African American contexts of care. She argues that healing cannot come for African Americans—and arguably for other marginalized and oppressed persons—without liberation from oppressive systems. Likewise, sustaining persons through times of turmoil is insufficient when fundamental questions of survival are at stake. Guidance—when predicated on perspectives shaped by white, male, heterosexual, or cisgender privilege—only exacerbates wounds of marginalization and oppression.[6] Likewise, reconciliation often fails to account for the oppressive relations of power between individuals and groups attempting to reconcile.

Thus Watkins Ali argues that the four classic functions of care have often failed to provide the nourishing and restorative care needed in situations of oppression. She adds to these the functions of *nurturing, empowering,* and *liberating* in order to develop pastoral care as a form of *"advocacy* that is embodied in action."[7] Specifically addressing African American experience, she argues, "To stay alive, and to stay in the struggle, many African Americans need a constant source of care that restores and replenishes vitality for continued resistance of the external oppressive circumstances."[8]

Nurturing care attempts to understand the experiences of suffering due to external oppressive circumstances in the lives of racial minorities toward the aim of bolstering the potential for survival and liberation through caregiving that takes into account the social context and political consequences of caring practices. We believe this applies to the care of women and LGBTQ people as well. The beginning stages of nurturing are demonstrated in the vignette of Helen, the transgender emergency room patient. Maria helped Helen to name her experience of microinvalidation of her gender identity in a way that was validating to her experience of microaggressive violence. Maria's care for Helen took up a nurturing function in Maria's attempt to understand Helen's experience and to communicate that understanding through language and actions that affirmed the importance of her experience of invalidation.

Watkins Ali calls the empowering function of pastoral care a search for ways "to enable persons to resist oppression on their own and to take authority over their own lives."[9] One of the important realities of empowerment, she argues, is that people who become empowered to address and resist oppression in their own lives are able to help other people become empowered. In the vignette of Cheryl and Anthony, Pastor Stanley was enacting an empowering function of care. Firstly, and perhaps most importantly, Pastor Stanley wasn't defensive about what he heard from Cheryl and Anthony about their experience at St. John's; instead, he responded proactively, empathizing with them and empowering a group in the congregation to address experiences of microaggressive violence. Upon assessing the dynamics of racial tokenism and microaggression in his own congregation and hearing Anthony and Cheryl attest to these dynamics, Pastor Stanley helped to build a coalition of support by empowering several white and African American members of the congregation with the self-awareness, skills, and community of allies needed in order to resist perpetrating the oppression of white privilege within the congregation. Pastor Stanley and the four congregants he spoke about to Cheryl and Anthony subsequently became important allies to them in their own experience of microaggression within the congregation.

Nadal argues that having allies during the experiences of discrimination— including microaggressive violence—benefits individuals for two reasons. First, allies help to validate the perceptions, feelings, and experiential realities of the person experiencing the microaggressions. Second, allies can join with the individual in practices of advocacy so that the individual experiencing the microaggressions doesn't have to address the situation alone.[10]

Finally, Watkins Ali suggests that liberating pastoral care must work toward liberation not only in an individual, psychological, or spiritual sense, but in a political sense as well.[11] "Liberating acts of ministry," she argues, "would be those that work toward actually setting persons free from oppression."[12] Maria helped Helen to advocate for her own rights as a patient in a way that honored Helen's desire to improve other transgender patients' experiences. Even more importantly, Maria engaged in practices of education and advocacy beyond her care for the individual, moving toward practices of pastoral advocacy with the potential for widespread institutional change.

As we follow the trajectory of the field of pastoral theology, care, and counseling beyond the predominance of the clinical paradigm into communal contextual and intercultural paradigms of care, the work of becoming a pastoral ally must lead to practices of care that account for the multiplicity of our socially constructed identities. Pastoral theologian Nancy J. Ramsay points to the framework of intersectionality as an increasingly important conceptual tool for pastoral caregivers to use in understanding the ways that hegemonic ideologies and stereotypes of human difference function on the macro level in the economic and political domains but also how they function on the micro level. Ramsay argues that it is at the micro level that "privilege and stigma are internalized by individuals who find their sense of themselves distorted by stereotypes that are at once inherently unachievable and powerfully operative in shaping our estimations of ourselves and others."[13]

Microaggressions are powerful carriers of this micro-level denigration, stigmatization, and stereotyping of human difference that hold the potential to operate violently against our deepest sense of self, or our soul. Therefore, pastoral care that is shaped by communal contextual and intercultural paradigms of care and that is operating to nurture, empower, and liberate in contexts of oppression and injustice must take into account the pervasive experience of microaggressive violence in everyday life, including in religious and theological contexts. Religious language and symbols not only have the capacity to uphold the social sins of racism, sexism, heterosexim, and genderism, but they have the capacity to *intensify* the strength of these oppressive social discourses by purporting to tell us who we are as individuals, in relation to others, and in relation to an ultimate reality. Thus in addition to *macro*-level assessments of microaggressions in our religious institutions, our practices of pastoral care and counseling must take into account how the social contexts of oppression operate on the *micro*-level of individual well-being and how caring practices can be extended through public theological advocacy to address the oppressive discourses in the social context as well.

Pastoral care and counseling have traditionally and rightly focused on the psychological, emotional, and spiritual experiences of distress among individuals. These are the practical disciplines most clearly dedicated to these concerns of human experience. But we must not be naive to the limitations of focusing on the psychological without attending to the social context of our lives. Drawing on the philosophy and theology of Martin Luther King Jr., pastoral theologian Donald M. Chinula argues that in order to fully understand and address psychic pain, trauma, and distress, it is vital to consider the concerns of overt and covert social strife. "This challenges pastoral caregiving to be as concerned about the health of the social psyche as it is about the human psyche," he argues.[14] Given our argument that microaggressions draw their strength to injure most deeply from their subtle citations of larger oppressive social discourses of racism, sexism, heterosexism, and genderism, pastoral caregivers wishing to address the pain and trauma caused by microaggressive violence must attend to both the social and individual psyches in practices of care.

Chinula suggests three practices that seem especially appropriate in addressing the impact of microaggressions in contexts of care and counseling: "This person-in-context approach asks both what is wrong with the sufferer and how he [or she] can be helped, as well as what might be wrong with the sufferer's setting and how altering the setting might change his [or her] symptomatic behavior."[15] In order to help pastoral caregivers attend to the person-in-context, he offers the four tasks of *reclamation, conciliation, transformation,* and *transcendence.*

Practices of reclamation attend the ways that a sense of self or identity is fractured by oppressive discourses as well as the ways they are carried by microaggressive communication.[16] In relation to LGBTQ persons, Sue argues, "Fragmentation or compartmentalization of the self results in feelings of isolation, alienation, and a possible sense of existential unreality about one's identity."[17] Pastoral care practices that attend carefully to the ways oppressive discourses attempt to split off certain pieces of one's sense of identity engage care seekers in a process of reclaiming those pieces. For example, in the second vignette in this chapter, the woman in the book study subtly communicates the need for this identity fragmentation by saying to Cheryl, a black woman, "I didn't see a black woman. I just saw a smart, attractive, accomplished woman." Pastor Stanley recognizes the violence in microaggressive statements like this one within the congregation, and he not only communicates empathic understanding to Cheryl but also works to influence the social psyche of the congregation to affect systemic change away from racial tokenism and "color-blind" ideologies.

Chinula also foregrounds from King's philosophy the practice of conciliation. He explains, "Conciliation differs from reconciliation in that its aim is to overcome the hostility or suspicion of the opponent."[18] This is extraordinarily important for practices of pastoral care in the communal context of congregations or religious institutions. Inevitably, we will all unintentionally and unknowingly communicate microaggressions toward people who embody difference in our communities. Confronting these microaggressive communications without providing any constructive methods to address our complicity in perpetrating them may lead to further practices of denial and the fragmentation of community, as those who experience these violent communications may then pull away for their own spiritual and emotional well-being. Pastoral practices of care that take seriously the need for conciliation are not satisfied merely with confrontation when these practices occur; instead, they require that pastoral practitioners lean in to these difficult, tension-filled experiences to inquire how, over time, the hostility, anxiety, and interpersonal pain created by microaggressions can be dissolved into "interpersonal and intergroup fellowship."[19] As demonstrated by Pastor Stanley, conciliatory pastoral practices attend to the ways that constructive confrontation of microaggressions is in service not only to the well-being of individuals but to the overall health of the community of faith.

In Chinula's constructive approach to King's philosophy, transformation "refers to changing the condition, nature, or character of persons and society so that the old is replaced by the new."[20] As in the case of Maria the chaplain, the pastoral practice of transformation took on two forms. First, Maria's use of the transgender patient's chosen, female name helped to transform Helen from an object into a beloved human being by witnessing and attesting to Helen's embodied experience as a transgender woman. Second, Maria helped to prompt the transformation of the social space of the hospital by tenaciously practicing pastoral advocacy for increased transgender education and patient rights.

Finally, Chinula offers the pastoral practice of transcendence to help practitioners discern ways of drawing on religious, spiritual, and theological resources to infuse the human spirit with the "inexhaustibility of divine reality" or that to which our symbols point to as of ultimate significance.[21] It is the inexhaustibility of the *imago Dei*, Chinula argues, that defies the ability of oppressive norms to define life for those targeted by oppression and microaggressive violence. Transcendence leads pastoral practitioners toward deeper understandings of the sense of ultimacy for care seekers — those theological narratives, symbols, and meanings that set life within an ultimate context, providing the materials out of which our deepest sense of self, our soul, emerges. Transcendence also leads pastoral caregivers to draw on the religious, spiritual, and theological narratives and themes central to the community of faith as a whole in order to construct an understanding of human community that embodies a fundamental regard for the *imago Dei* expressed in the varied embodiments of human difference. Just as theological and spiritual narratives and symbols hold the potential to gravely intensify the harm of microaggressions in ministerial contexts, so do theological and spiritual narratives and symbols offer pastoral practitioners vital tools for the continued cultivation of communities characterized by an ethic of care for both the individual psyche and the social psyche.

Conclusion

*T*hroughout this book, we have shown how the context of theological narratives, language, and symbols deepen the already damaging impact of microaggressions on oppressed persons. We have also shown the potential that exists within faith communities to promote resistance and resilience in the face of microaggressive violence. Beginning by constructing a theological approach to microaggressions, we examined the roles of microaggressions addressed at persons of color, women, and LGBTQs within faith settings in part 1. In part 2, we offered tools for addressing microaggressions within preaching and education, worship and spirituality, pastoral care and counseling. Now we would like to return briefly to why we chose to write this book.

Cody's Closing Thoughts

At the end of this lengthy project, I continue to find meaning in the words I penned at its outset. This book is a labor of love for the church and an act of taking responsibility for my own place within it as a minister ordained to care for congregations and communities of faith. In order to follow my own vocational sense of call, in order to honor my own deeply held sentiment of love for the church, I cannot ignore the potential of our religious institutions to unnecessarily perpetuate microaggressive violence against the most vulnerable in our congregations. I also dream of an awakening taking place among the laypersons and clergypersons reading this book—an awakening to all of the ways that churches and religious institutions can cease perpetuating microaggressive violence as well as the ways that our communities of faith may become sources of resistance and resilience in the face of microaggressions in the larger society.

Angela's Closing Thoughts

The process of writing this book has been both illuminating and disheartening. Doing research and listening to the stories of other marginalized people who have experienced microaggressions within the confines of faith communities has taught me a great deal about the intersections among justice, power, privilege, equality, and the gospel. I have been called out and held accountable for my own unjust actions. I have experienced solidarity in learning about the experiences of other women and LGBTQs, knowing that I am not alone in my struggles with the church. For both of these things, I am tremendously grateful.

At the same time, both research and listening to others have broken my heart again and again. That the church, theology, Scripture, denominational polity, or seminary classrooms have been used as bludgeons for battering the souls of so many marginalized people is simply unacceptable. The psychological, emotional, spiritual, and physical strain that microaggressions have placed on so many of God's beloved children is too much to bear. The fact that these very microaggressions continue to thrive within faith communities is something we can tolerate no longer.

Throughout the research and writing process, I have claimed many times that thoughtfully addressing microaggressions within faith communities may be my last hope for the church. The wounds are too deep and too far-reaching, and they impact too many people for me to sit idly by as a queer clergyperson. The time has come to act, to include, to listen, to learn, and to overcome together. Skeptically hopeful, I remain on the fringes of faith, clinging to the calling we all share: to do justice, love kindness, walk humbly.

Who Is Missing?

Throughout our research, we have encouraged churches, denominations, seminaries, and individual persons of faith to ask how their words and actions impact the least among us. We limited our discussion to three groups who are often treated as being in that category: persons of color, women, and LGBTQs. Still, because there are many others who experience microaggressions within faith communities, we have much work to do. It is imperative that we expand our work on microaggressions in ministry to include ableism, fatphobia, classism, xenophobia, and ageism. Though we have touched on some of these issues in a very cursory way, we hope to expand the current focus of this book to also include these perspectives in our future research, writing, and presentations.

Whether you are clergy, laity, professor, seminarian, or some combination of these various identities, we hope that you will take the knowledge you have gleaned from this book into the world. Preach about the power of microaggressions to harm. Attend to them in the music and the liturgy of the church. Teach about them in Sunday school, in seminary, and in religious studies classrooms. Incorporate this awareness into your spiritual disciplines. Utilize this knowledge in your pastoral care and counseling. Commit to transforming churches, denominations, and seminaries into places where all people are welcomed, affirmed, included, and celebrated in their innumerable, exciting, multifaceted diversity. Commit to creating such a world inside and outside of the confines of faith.

Benediction

Galvanized by the knowledge that your theological narratives, language, and symbols hold the power to assault the souls of countless oppressed persons, go forth to expand your narratives so that they affirm the marginalized, broadening your language so that it includes the least among us, and reenvisioning your symbols so that they celebrate the beautiful diversity of humankind.

Inspired by a God whose love is all-encompassing, expansive, never ending, passionate, and radically inclusive, go forth to embody such love in your actions—your preaching, teaching, worship, spirituality, pastoral care, and counseling—so that all people within your reach may know how deeply they are loved.

Emboldened by the faith that you too are deeply loved, go forth to love others in such a way that justice is actualized, compassion is felt, inclusion is known, and grace is enlivened by your every word and deed. May it be so. Amen.

Notes

CHAPTER 1: INTRODUCING MICROAGGRESSIONS

1. Derald Wing Sue, *Microaggressions in Everyday Life: Race, Gender, and Sexual Orientation* (Hoboken, NJ: Wiley, 2010), xvi. Also see Pierce, Charles M., Jean V. Carew, Diane Pierce-Gonzalez, and Deborah Willis, "An Experiment in Racism: TV Commercials," in *Television and Education*, ed. Charles Pierce (Beverly Hills, CA: SAGE, 1978), 62–88.

2. Though Sue has authored and coauthored numerous journal articles and book chapters on microaggressions, his primary single-author text on the subject to which we most often refer is *Microaggressions in Everyday Life.*

3. Kevin L. Nadal, *That's So Gay! Microaggressions and the Lesbian, Gay, Bisexual, and Transgender Community* (Washington, DC: American Psychological Association, 2013), 6.

4. Sue, *Microaggressions in Everyday Life*, xv.

5. Gilles Deleuze, as quoted in Michel Foucault, "Intellectuals and Power: A Conversation between Michel Foucault and Gilles Deleuze," in *Language, Counter-Memory, Practice*, ed. Donald F. Bouchard, trans. Donald F. Bouchard and Sherry Simon (Ithaca, NY: Cornell University Press, 1977), 208.

6. Namson Kang, *Cosmopolitan Theology: Reconstituting Planetary Hospitality, Neighbor-Love, and Solidarity in an Uneven World* (St. Louis: Chalice, 2013), 2.

7. Sue, *Microaggressions in Everyday Life*, xvi.

8. While this text focuses primarily upon microaggressions targeting persons based on race, gender, sexual orientation, or gender identity, we encourage those interested in furthering their exploration to class, ability, and religion to see the following essays from Derald Wing Sue, ed., *Microaggressions and Marginality: Manifestation, Dynamics, and Impact* (Hoboken, NJ: Wiley, 2010): Richard M. Keller and Corinne E. Galgay, "Microaggressive Experiences of People with Disabilities," 241–67; Laura Smith and Rebecca M. Redington. "Class Dismissed: Making the Case for the Study of Classist Microaggressions," 269–85; and Kevin L. Nadal, Marie-Anne Issa, Katie E. Griffin, Sahran Hamit, and Oliver Lyons, "Religious Microaggressions in the United States: Mental Health Implications for Religious Minority Groups," 287–310.

9. Sue, *Microaggressions in Everyday Life*, xv.

10. Ibid., 41.

11. Henry A. Giroux, *Pedagogy and the Politics of Hope: Theory, Culture, and Schooling* (Boulder, CO: Westview, 1997), 6.

12. Sue, *Microaggressions in Everyday Life*, 31.

13. Ibid., 37.

14. For more on the "perpetual foreigner" experience for Latino/a persons, see David P. Rivera, Erin E. Forquer, and Rebecca Rangel, "Microaggressions and the Life Experience of Latina/o Americans," in Sue, ed., *Microaggressions and Marginality*, 72. This is a microin-validation often experienced by Asian Americans as well.

15. Sue, *Microaggressions in Everyday Life*, 28.

16. Ibid., 29–30.

17. See ibid., 108; Nadal, *That's So Gay!*, 229.

18. Sue, *Microaggressions in Everyday Life*, 40.

19. Ibid., 114.

20. Ibid., 50.

21. Derald Wing Sue, "Microaggressions, Marginality, and Oppression: An Introduction," in Sue, ed., *Microaggressions and Marginality*, 11.

22. Sue states that decreasing defensiveness allows us to become more attentive to the experience of marginalized groups and diminishes the power of the false reality perpetuated by sexism, racism, heterosexism, and genderism in society. Sue, *Microaggressions in Everyday Life*, 128.

23. Sue, "Microaggressions, Marginality, and Oppression," 17.

24. Sue, *Microaggressions in Everyday Life*, 54.

25. Nadal, *That's So Gay!*, 158.

26. Ibid.

27. Ibid.

28. Ibid., 160.

29. Sue, *Microaggressions in Everyday Life*, 81.

30. Ibid., 89.

31. Nadal, Kevin L., Yinglee Wong, Marie-Anne Issa, Vanessa Meterko, Jayleen Leon, and Michelle Wideman, "Sexual Orientation Microaggressions: Processes and Coping Mechanisms for Lesbian, Gay, and Bisexual Individuals," *Journal of LGBT Issues in Counseling* 5 (2011): 155–56.

32. While Sue's scholarship on microaggressions is generally highly regarded and frequently cited in the psychological literature on multicultural competence, we should note that the theory of microaggressions also has a number of detractors. For example, Goodstein cites Sue's blurring of "the distinction between racial groups and culture" (276) and the possibility of misrepresenting how people actually make self-identifications with racial or cultural groups. In addition, Goodstein argues that Sue's exploration of microaggressions privileges race in a hierarchical paradigm of suffering, thereby diminishing the importance of other forms of microaggressions based on gender, sexual orientation, physical ability, etc. See Renée Goodstein, "What's Missing from the Dialogue on Racial Microaggressions in Counseling and Therapy," *American Psychologist* 63, no. 4 (2008): 276–77.

On a different note, Schacht challenges Sue and his collaborators on their ability to name one person in a dyad as the "perpetrator" of the microaggressive interaction, believing this to be one-sided in its refusal to acknowledge that each person in the dyad "acts and reacts, remembers and constructs, projects and internalizes, in a complex, cyclical, and recursive interpersonal and psychodynamic dance that defies simple reductive description or ascription of responsibility to one actor" (273). Thomas E. Schacht, "A Broader View of Racial Microaggressions in Psychotherapy," *American Psychologist* 63, no. 4 (2008): 273.

Finally, Thomas argues that Sue and colleagues are misleading in their attribution of micro-aggressions to racial slights rather than acknowledging that, regardless of race, anyone may expect to experience verbal, behavioral, or environmental indignities. Further, he posits that Sue and his associates are advocating "restrictions on normal human interaction" that "could have a chilling effect on free speech and on the willingness of White people . . . to interact with people of color" (274). See Kenneth R. Thomas, "Macrononsense in Multiculturalism," *American Psychologist* 63, no. 4 (2008): 274–75.

33. Sue, *Microaggressions in Everyday Life*, 91.

34. Sue, "Microaggressions, Marginality, and Oppression," 14.

35. Christine M. Smith, *Preaching as Weeping, Confession, and Resistance: Radical Responses to Radical Evil* (Louisville, KY: Westminster John Knox, 1992), 5.

CHAPTER 2: ASSAILING THE SOUL

1. Derald Wing Sue, *Microaggressions in Everyday Life: Race, Gender, and Sexual Orientation* (Hoboken, NJ: Wiley, 2010), xvi.

2. Lucy Atkinson Rose, *Sharing the Word: Preaching in the Roundtable Church* (Louisville, KY: Westminster John Knox, 1997), 90.

3. For further discussion of the responsibility ministers have in attending to the ways theological language can uphold practices of domination, oppression, and violence, see Rebecca Chopp, *The Power to Speak: Feminism, Language, God* (Eugene, OR: Wipf & Stock, 2002).

4. Judith Butler, *Excitable Speech: A Politics of the Performative* (New York: Routledge, 1997), 1–2.

5. See Raymond Martin and John Barresi, *The Rise and Fall of Soul and Self: An Intellectual History of Personal Identity* (New York: Columbia University Press, 2006), and Stewart Goetz and Charles Taliaferro, *A Brief History of the Soul* (Hoboken, NJ: Wiley-Blackwell, 2011).

6. "Other-seeking agent" is a term used by James A. Holsetin and Jaber F. Gubrium in *The Self We Live By: Narrative Identity in a Postmodern World* (New York: Oxford University Press, 2000), 10.

7. Charles Taylor, *Sources of the Self: The Making of Modern Identity* (Cambridge, MA: Harvard University Press, 1989), 35.

8. James R. Farris, "The Ontology of Violence," in *Pastoral Theology's and Pastoral Psychology's Contributions to Helping Heal a Violent World*, ed. G. Michael Cordner (Surakarta, Indonesia: International Pastoral Care Network for Social Responsibility and DABARA Publishers, 1996), 120.

9. C. Allen Carter, *Kenneth Burke and the Scapegoat Process* (Norman, OK: University of Oklahoma Press, 1996), xvii–xviii.

10. Gordon D. Kaufman, *In Face of Mystery: A Constructive Theology* (Cambridge, MA: Harvard University Press, 1993), 77.

11. Farris, "Ontology of Violence," 122.

12. Kaufman, *In Face of Mystery*, 77.

13. Farris, "Ontology of Violence," 119.

14. Didier Eribon, *Insult and the Making of the Gay Self*, trans. Michael Lucey (Durham, NC: Duke University Press, 2004), 98–99.

15. In a survey of 6,450 transgender and gender-nonconforming persons, one-fifth (19 percent) reported experiencing homelessness because of their transgender or gender-nonconforming identity, and 55 percent of those who tried to access a homeless shelter were

harassed by shelter staff or other residents, 29 percent were completely turned away from the shelters altogether, and 22 percent were sexually assaulted by staff or other residents. In addition, like Brad in our vignette, 57 percent of participants in the survey experienced significant family rejection. See Jaime M. Grant, Lisa A. Mottet, and Justin Tanis, *Injustice at Every Turn: A Report of the National Transgender Discrimination Survey* (Washington, DC: National Center for Transgender Equality and National Gay and Lesbian Task Force, 2011), http://endtransdiscrimination.org/PDFs/NTDS_Report.pdf.

CHAPTER 3: MICROAGGRESSIONS AND RACE

1. CPE is the standard training process for persons wishing to become certified as chaplains and to serve in settings such as hospitals and hospices. It involves working in a clinical context and coming together with CPE peers and a supervisor regularly to engage in theologically reflective dialogue on one's clinical work, professional relationships, and ministerial identity formation.

2. The definition of racism as "a system of advantage based on race" is from David T. Wellman, *Portraits of White Racism* (New York: Cambridge University Press, 1977), as cited in Beverly Daniel Tatum, "Talking about Race, Learning about Racism: The Application of Racial Identity Development Theory in the Classroom," *Harvard Educational Review* 62, no. 1 (1992): 3.

3. Eleazar Fernandez posits, "White sin is the elevation of whiteness to the status of normativity, and the regulation of other colors to deviancy." Eleazar S. Fernandez, *Reimagining the Human: Theological Anthropology in Response to Systemic Evil* (St. Louis: Chalice, 2004), 146.

4. Ibid., 138.

5. Ibid., 153.

6. Peggy McIntosh, "White Privilege: Unpacking the Invisible Knapsack," in *Multiculturalism, 1992*, ed. Anna May Filor (New York State Council of Educational Associations, 1992), 30. This essay is a helpful, engaging introduction to white privilege for use in congregations and the classroom.

7. Derald Wing Sue and David Sue, *Counseling the Culturally Diverse: Theory and Practice*, 5th ed. (Hoboken, NJ: Wiley, 2007), as cited in Nicole Watkins, Theressa L. Labarrie, and Lauren M. Appio, "Black Undergraduates' Experiences with Perceived Racial Microaggressions in Predominately White Colleges and Universities," in *Microaggressions and Marginality: Manifestation, Dynamics, and Impact*, ed. Derald Wing Sue (Hoboken, NJ: Wiley, 2010), 26.

8. Emilie M. Townes, *Womanist Ethics and the Cultural Production of Evil* (New York: Palgrave Macmillan, 2006), 19–20.

9. Frances E. Kendall, *Understanding White Privilege: Creating Pathways to Authentic Relationships Across Race* (New York: Routledge, 2006), 63.

10. Ibid., 69.

11. Three texts addressing the intersection of race and sexual orientation that are helpful for discussions in congregation and classroom are Kelly Brown Douglas, *Sexuality and the Black Church: A Womanist Perspective* (Maryknoll, NY: Orbis, 1999); Patrick S. Cheng, *Rainbow Theology: Bridging Race, Sexuality, and Spirit* (New York: Seabury, 2013); and Horace L. Griffin, *Their Own Receive Them Not: African American Lesbians and Gays in Black Churches* (Cleveland: Pilgrim, 2006). In addition, ethicist Keri Day addresses the intersection of black women and socioeconomic class in *Unfinished Business: Black*

Women, the Black Church, and the Struggle to Thrive in America (Maryknoll, NY: Orbis, 2012).

12. Kendall, *Understanding White Privilege*, 105.

13. A helpful resource for addressing white privilege/supremacy in churches and religious institutions is Jennifer Harvey, Karin A. Case, and Robin Hawley, eds., *Disrupting White Supremacy from Within: White People on What We Need To Do* (Cleveland: Pilgrim, 2004).

14. James R. Farris, "The Ontology of Violence," in *Pastoral Theology's and Pastoral Psychology's Contributions to Helping Heal a Violent World*, ed. G. Michael Cordner (Surakarta, Indonesia: International Pastoral Care Network for Social Responsibility and DABARA Publishers, 1996), 122.

15. Derald Wing Sue, *Microaggressions in Everyday Life: Race, Gender, and Sexual Orientation* (Hoboken, NJ: Wiley, 2010), 38.

16. Fumitaka Matsuoka, *The Color of Faith: Building Community in a Multiracial Society* (Cleveland: United Church Press, 1998), 19.

17. Fernandez, *Reimagining the Human*, 142.

18. Kendall, *Understanding White Privilege*, 51.

19. Matsuoka, *Color of Faith*, 4.

20. Ibid.

21. Matsuoka draws the notion of "monopoly of imagination" from Robert Merton, *Social Theology and Social Structure* (Glencoe, IL: Free Press, 1957).

22. Sue, *Microaggressions in Everyday Life*, 128.

23. Matsuoka, *Color of Faith*, 55–56.

24. Kendall, *Understanding White Privilege*, 129.

25. David P. Rivera, Erin E. Forquer, and Rebecca Rangel, "Microaggressions and the Life Experience of Latina/o Americans," in *Microaggressions and Marginality: Manifestation, Dynamics, and Impact*, ed. Derald Wing Sue (Hoboken, NJ: Wiley, 2010), 73.

26. Ibid., 76.

27. Annie I. Lin, "Racial Microaggressions Directed at Asian Americans: Modern Forms of Prejudice and Discrimination," in *Microaggressions and Marginality: Manifestation, Dynamics, and Impact*, ed. Derald Wing Sue (Hoboken, NJ: Wiley, 2010), 92.

28. Rivera, Forquer, and Rangel, "Microaggressions and the Life Experience of Latina/o Americans," 76.

29. Kevin L. Nadal, *That's So Gay! Microaggressions and the Lesbian, Gay, Bisexual, and Transgender Community* (Washington, DC: American Psychological Association, 2013), 157.

30. Ibid., 160.

31. Ibid., 159.

32. Matsuoka, *Color of Faith*, 53.

33. Tatum, "Talking about Race, Learning about Racism," 20.

34. Patricia Hill Collins, *On Intellectual Activism* (Philadelphia: Temple University Press, 2013), 128.

35. Townes, *Womanist Ethics and the Cultural Production of Evil*, 23.

36. Kendall, *Understanding White Privilege*, 47.

37. Matsuoka, *Color of Faith*, 49.

38. Townes, *Womanist Ethics and the Cultural Production of Evil*, 27.

39. Ibid. These practices are supported by the microaggressions research in higher education in which Watkins, Labarrie, and Appio found that while "Black students tend to feel more confident and validated as racial beings when they are encouraged to foster a critical

racial consciousness, it follows that White professors' avoidance of these topics is highly disadvantageous to the coping abilities of students of color, as well as to the education of White students, who may unknowingly perpetuate subtle forms of oppression." Watkins, Labarrie, and Appio, "Black Undergraduates' Experiences with Perceived Racial Microaggressions," 45.

40. Townes, *Womanist Ethics and the Cultural Production of Evil*, 114.

41. We are indebted to Patrick Cheng for encouraging us to consider how churches equip people to address the microaggressions they experience in the wider world.

42. Matsuoka, *Color of Faith*, 61.

43. Ibid., 62.

44. M. Shawn Copeland, *Enfleshing Freedom: Body, Race, and Being* (Minneapolis: Fortress, 2010), 94.

45. For a discussion of these common responses, see Tatum, "Talking about Race, Learning about Racism."

46. Kendall, *Understanding White Privilege*, 32–33.

CHAPTER 4: MICROAGGRESSIONS AND GENDER

1. See Luce Irigaray, *This Sex Which Is Not One* (Ithaca, NY: Cornell University Press, 1985).

2. Thomas Aquinas, *Summa theologica* 1, q.92, a.1, ad 1.

3. Derald Wing Sue, *Microaggressions in Everyday Life: Race, Gender, and Sexual Orientation* (Hoboken, NJ: Wiley, 2010), 177.

4. United States Department of Labor, "Labor Force Statistics from the Current Population Survey," http://www.bls.gov/cps/wlf-databook2006.htm.

5. Derald Wing Sue, *Microaggressions in Everyday Life: Race, Gender, and Sexual Orientation* (Hoboken, NJ: Wiley, 2010), 168.

6. Ibid.

7. Ibid., 169–76.

8. Sharon Warner, "The Value of Particularity: Inclusive Language Revisted," *Lexington Theological Quarterly* 29 (Winter 1994): 249.

9. Ibid., 251.

10. Karen Leigh Stroup, "God Our Mother: A Call to Truly Inclusive Language," *Lexington Theological Quarterly* 27 (January 1992): 12–13.

11. Marjorie Procter-Smith, *In Her Own Rite: Constructing Feminist Liturgical Tradition* (Nashville: Order of Saint Luke's Publishing, 1990), 91.

12. Warner, "Value of Particularity," 257.

13. Ibid.

14. Sue, *Microaggressions in Everyday Life*, 173.

15. Ibid., 174.

16. Kevin L. Nadal, *That's So Gay! Microaggressions and the Lesbian, Gay, Bisexual, and Transgender Community* (Washington, DC: American Psychological Association, 2013), 160.

17. Sue, *Microaggressions in Everyday Life*, 176.

18. Ibid., 178.

19. Ibid., 180.

20. April DeConick, *Holy Misogyny: Why the Sex and Gender Conflicts in the Early Church Still Matter* (New York: Continuum, 2011), 151–52.

CHAPTER 5: MICROAGGRESSIONS AND SEXUAL ORIENTATION AND GENDER IDENTITY

1. Even since the 2009 signing of the Matthew Shepard and James Byrd Jr. Hate Crimes Prevention Act into federal law, the violent attack and murder of lesbian, gay, bisexual, and transgender persons—as well as many who are simply presumed to be LGBTQ—continues to cast an ominous pall over U.S. society. The National Coalition of Anti-Violence Programs reports that in 2011, there was an overall decrease of 16 percent in reports of hate violence against lesbian, gay, bisexual, transgender, queer, and HIV-affected persons. While this news seems consoling, this same report includes the highest number of hate-motivated murders ever recorded by this organization, with people under the age of thirty most likely to be targeted. See the National Coalition of Anti-Violence Programs, *Hate Violence Against Lesbian, Gay, Bisexual, Transgender, Queer, and HIV-affected Communities in the United States in 2011* (New York: New York City Gay & Lesbian Anti-Violence Project, 2012), accessible at http://www.avp.org/storage/documents/Reports/2012_NCAVP_2011_HV _Report.pdf.

2. Gary Gates notes that in the United States, around 4 percent of the adult population are LGBT. Illustrating the dramatic disparity in homelessness among LGBT people, a 2010 report by the Center for American Progress reports that in many U.S. cities, between 15 percent and 40 percent of the homeless youth population identify as LGBTQ. See Gary J. Gates, "How Many People Are Lesbian, Gay, Bisexual, and Transgender?" research brief, Williams Institute, UCLA School of Law, April 2011, accessible at http:// williamsinstitute.law.ucla.edu/wp-content/uploads/Gates-How-Many-People-LGBT-Apr -2011.pdf. See also Nico Sifra Quintana, Josh Rosenthal, and Jeff Krehely, "On the Streets: The Federal Response to Gay and Transgender Homeless Youth," report, Center for American Progress, June 2010, accessible at http://cdn.americanprogress.org/wp-content/uploads/ issues/2010/06/pdf/lgbtyouthhomelessness.pdf. For information on churches addressing LGBTQ youth homelessness, see Cody J. Sanders, "Homeless LGBTQ Youth and Progressive Churches: A New Agenda for Care and Justice," *Huffington Post*, September 9, 2014, http:// www.huffingtonpost.com/rev-cody-j-sanders/homeless-lgbtq-youth-progressive-churches _b_5780922.html.

3. Kevin L. Nadal, *That's So Gay! Microaggressions and the Lesbian, Gay, Bisexual, and Transgender Community* (Washington, DC: American Psychological Association, 2013) 46–47. Nadal is drawing upon an earlier iteration of this taxonomy he developed in Kevin L. Nadal, David P. Rivera, and Melissa J. H. Corpus, "Sexual Orientation and Transgender Microaggressions in Everyday Life: Experiences of Lesbians, Gays, Bisexuals, and Transgender Individuals," in *Microaggressions and Marginality: Manifestation, Dynamics, and Impact*, ed. Derald Wing Sue (New York: Wiley, 2010), 217–40.

4. Nadal, *That's So Gay*, 46.

5. Ibid.

6. Ibid., 61.

7. Ibid., 46.

8. Ibid.

9. Ibid.

10. Ibid., 46–7.

11. Ibid., 47.

12. Ibid., 118–22.

13. U.S. Department of Health and Human Services (HHS) Office of the Surgeon General and National Action Alliance for Suicide Prevention, *2012 National Strategy for Suicide Prevention: Goals and Objectives for Action* (Washington, DC: HHS, 2012), 101.

14. Ibid., 121.

15. Jaime M. Grant, Lisa A. Mottet, and Justin Tanis, *Injustice at Every Turn: A Report of the National Transgender Discrimination Survey* (Washington, DC: National Center for Transgender Equality and National Gay and Lesbian Task Force, 2011), 1.

16. Derald Wing Sue, *Microaggressions in Everyday Life: Race, Gender, and Sexual Orientation* (Hoboken, NJ: Wiley, 2010), 199–200.

17. Ibid., 200.

18. Didier Eribon, *Insult and the Making of the Gay Self*, trans. Michael Lucey (Durham, NC: Duke University Press, 2004), 98–99.

19. Iris Marion Young, *Justice and the Politics of Difference* (Princeton, NJ: Princeton University Press, 1990), 62.

20. For more on the politics of disgust in relation to sexual orientation, see Martha C. Nussbaum, *From Disgust to Humanity: Sexual Orientation and Constitutional Law* (New York: Oxford University Press, 2010).

21. Derald Wing Sue, *Microaggressions in Everyday Life: Race, Gender, and Sexual Orientation* (Hoboken, NJ: Wiley, 2010), 89.

22. Ibid.

23. Lucy Atkinson Rose, *Sharing the Word: Preaching in the Roundtable Church* (Louisville, KY: Westminster John Knox, 1997), 127.

24. In lists such as these, when "gender" is named, this is not indicative of persons of diverse gender *identities*. Gender typically references the male and female binary. Churches wishing to communicate the welcome and inclusion of transgender, intersex, and genderqueer people should also name the human experience of "gender identity" in such lists as well.

25. "Ze" is a gender-neutral pronoun to replace "he" and "she" that can be used without implying anything about a person's gender. This and other neologisms are variously used by persons not ascribing to the gender binary system, while others simply prefer to be referred to by their proper name rather than with a pronoun or, at times, with the plural pronouns "they/them." Churches wishing to explore ministry with transgender persons should consult Justin Tanis, *Trans-Gendered: Theology, Ministry, and Communities of Faith* (Cleveland: Pilgrim, 2003).

26. Patrick Cheng, *Rainbow Theology: Bridging Race, Sexuality, and Spirit* (New York: Seabury, 2013), 89.

27. Ibid., 91.

28. Ibid., 138.

29. Cheng, *Rainbow Theology*, 90.

CHAPTER 6: MICROAGGRESSIONS IN WORD

1. Some of the material represented in this chapter first took shape in Cody J. Sanders, "Preaching Messages We Never Intended: LGBTQ-Based Microaggressions in Classroom and Pulpit," *Theology and Sexuality* 19, no. 1 (2013): 21–35.

2. Lucy Atkinson Rose, *Sharing the Word: Preaching in the Roundtable Church* (Louisville, KY: Westminster John Knox, 1997).

3. Robert E. C. Browne, *The Ministry of the Word* (London: SCM Press, 1958), 73, cited in Rose, *Sharing the Word*, 90.

4. Joseph Sittler, *The Anguish of Preaching* (Philadelphia: Fortress, 1966), 55, cited in Rose, *Sharing the Word*, 91.

5. Rose, *Sharing the Word*, 90.

6. Ibid., 97.

7. Rebecca Chopp, *The Power to Speak: Feminism, Language, God* (Eugene, OR: Wipf & Stock, 2002), 103.

8. Ibid., 6–7.

9. Christine M. Smith, *Preaching as Weeping, Confession, and Resistance: Radical Responses to Radical Evil* (Louisville, KY: Westminster John Knox, 1992), 2.

10. John S. McClure, *Other-Wise Preaching: A Postmodern Ethic for Homiletics* (St. Louis: Chalice, 2001), 7.

11. Rose, *Sharing the Word*, 127.

12. Derald Wing Sue, *Microaggressions in Everyday Life: Race, Gender, and Sexual Orientation* (Hoboken, NJ: Wiley, 2010), 55.

13. McClure, *Other-Wise Preaching*, 234.

14. Sue, *Microaggressions in Everyday Life*, 40.

15. Kevin L. Nadal, *That's So Gay! Microaggressions and the Lesbian, Gay, Bisexual, and Transgender Community* (Washington, DC: American Psychological Association, 2013), 159.

16. Ibid., 164.

17. Ibid., 179.

18. Ibid., 186.

19. Sue, *Microaggressions in Everyday Life*, 106.

CHAPTER 7: MICROAGGRESSIONS IN MUSIC, SPACE, AND PRAYER

1. For more on particular inclusive language, see Sharon Warner, "The Value of Particularity: Inclusive Language Revisted," *Lexington Theological Quarterly 29*, no. 4 (Winter 1994).

2. Fumitaka Matsuoka, *The Color of Faith: Building Community in a Multiracial Society* (Cleveland: United Church Press, 1998), 4.

3. M. Shawn Copeland, *Enfleshing Freedom: Body, Race, and Being* (Minneapolis: Fortress, 2010), 82.

4. Elizabeth Stuart, "Sacramental Flesh," in *Queer Theology: Rethinking the Western Body*, ed. Gerard Loughlin (Malden, MA: Blackwell, 2007), 66.

5. Ibid., 68.

6. See Lloyd Sheldon Johnson, "Spirituality as a Viable Resource in Responding to Racial Microaggressions: An Exploratory Study of Black Males Who Attended a Community College," doctoral dissertation, University of Massachusetts Boston (June 2012).

7. Such research not only exists in medical journals, but it has also become popular in an array of contemporary magazines, such as *Fitness, Shape, Prevention,* and *O, The Oprah Magazine.*

8. Johnson, "Spirituality as a Viable Resource," 39.

9. For more on the spiritual pedagogy of multiculturalism, see Kathleen Talvacchia, *Critical Minds and Discerning Hearts: A Spirituality of Multicultural Teaching* (St. Louis: Chalice, 2003).

CHAPTER 8: MICROAGGRESSIONS IN PASTORAL RELATIONSHIPS

1. See Derald Wing Sue, *Microaggressions in Everyday Life: Race, Gender, and Sexual Orientation* (Hoboken, NJ: Wiley, 2010), 38.

2. Nancy J. Ramsay, "A Time of Ferment and Redefinition," in *Pastoral Care and Counseling: Redefining the Paradigms,* ed. Nancy J. Ramsay (Nashville: Abingdon, 2004), 9.

3. Ibid., 11. See John Patton, *Pastoral Care in Context: An Introduction to Pastoral Care* (Louisville, KY: Westminster John Knox, 1993), and Larry Kent Graham, *Care of Persons, Care of Worlds: A Psychosystems Approach to Care and Counseling* (Nashville: Abingdon, 1992).

4. Ramsay, "A Time of Ferment and Redefinition," 12, 35. See Emmanuel Y. Lartey, *In Living Color: An Intercultural Approach to Pastoral Care and Counseling,* 2nd ed. (Philadelphia: Jessica Kingsley, 2003).

5. William A. Clebsch and Charles R. Jaekle, *Pastoral Care in Historical Perspective: An Essay with Exhibits* (Englewood Cliffs, NJ: Prentice-Hall, 1964), 8–9.

6. Carroll A. Watkins Ali, *Survival and Liberation: Pastoral Theology in African American Context* (St. Louis: Chalice, 1999), 138. For literature that addresses a multiplicity of embodiments of human difference with an orientation toward informing practices of care with a social justice lens, see Sheryl A. Kujawa-Holbrook and Karen B. Montagno, eds., *Injustice and the Care of Souls: Taking Oppression Seriously in Pastoral Care* (Minneapolis: Fortress, 2009).

7. Watkins Ali, *Survival and Liberation,* 9, 137.

8. Ibid., 139.

9. Ibid.

10. Kevin L. Nadal, *That's So Gay! Microaggressions and the Lesbian, Gay, Bisexual, and Transgender Community* (Washington, DC: American Psychological Association, 2013), 77.

11. The literature developing pastoral theology and care as a discipline of political, liberative engagement is now quite extensive and seemingly underutilized by practitioners of ministry. See Homer U. Ashby Jr., "Pastoral Theology as Public Theology: Participating in the Healing of Damaged and Damaging Cultures and Institutions," *Journal of Pastoral Theology* 10 (2000): 18–27; Larry Kent Graham, "Pastoral Theology as Public Theology in Relation to the Clinic," *Journal of Pastoral Theology* 10 (2000): 1–17; and *Pastoral Psychology* 64, no. 4 (2014), a special issue dedicated to the theme "Pastoral Care and Politics" and edited by Ryan LaMothe and Bruce Rogers-Vaughn.

12. Watkins Ali, *Survival and Liberation,* 140.

13. Nancy J. Ramsay, "Intersectionality: A Model for Addressing the Complexity of Oppression and Privilege," *Pastoral Psychology* 63, no. 4 (2014): 458–59.

14. Donald M. Chinula, *Building King's Beloved Community: Foundations for Pastoral Care and Counseling with the Oppressed* (Eugene, OR: Wipf & Stock, 1997), 62.

15. Ibid., 68.

16. Ibid., 56–57.

17. Sue, *Microaggressions in Everyday Life,* 199.

18. Chinula, *Building King's Beloved Community,* 57.

19. Ibid., 57.

20. Ibid.

21. Ibid., 58.

Glossary

DEFINITION OF TERMS RELATED TO MICROAGGRESSIONS

attributional ambiguity: Uncertainty over motives and meanings of a person's microaggressive action. From the perspective of those targeted by microaggressions, it is often unclear whether or not a microaggressive communication is intentional or whether it means to the perpetrator what it seems to mean to the target.

environmental microaggression: Elements within organizations, systems, or institutions—such as the arrangement of physical space, institutional norms, or corporate practices—that serve to insult or denigrate persons based on an embodiment of human difference or to invalidate the experience of minority group members.

intersectional microaggression: A microaggression that targets a person based on the intersection of multiple markers of identity, such as the person's race and sexual orientation, gender and class, etc.

metacommunication: Cues such as verbal tone, inflection, and visual gestures that indicate to a hearer how spoken words and phrases are to be interpreted. The message communicated by metacommunication can be at odds with the content of the spoken words themselves, thus producing ambiguity as to just what message is being communicated.

microaggression: Brief and often subtle everyday verbal or visual exchanges or environmental cues that send denigrating messages to certain individuals because of their group membership based on markers of human difference, including race, gender, sexual orientation, gender identity, age, ability, religion, and ethnic or national heritage.

microassault: Most often a conscious and intentional exchange intended to communicate a demeaning attack or inflict harm based on a target's embodiment of human difference, such as race, gender, sexual orientation, or gender identity.

microinsult: Most often an unconscious and unintentional exchange that communicates stereotypes, rudeness, and insensitivity toward an embodiment of human difference, such as race, gender sexual orientation, or gender identity.

microinvalidation: Most often an unconscious and unintentional exchange that serves to deny the validity of personal experiences by invalidating, negating, or excluding thoughts, feelings, and experiential realities of the targeted party.

power: In discussions of microaggressions, power typically indicates the ability to define reality through language, media, and institutional norms based on the experience of dominant majority perspectives and life experiences rather than by physical or coercive power.

privilege: The unearned favorable, personally advantageous experiences of those in dominant racial, gender, or sexual orientation groups afforded to persons based solely on those markers of identity (e.g., white, male, heterosexual).

DEFINITION OF TERMS RELATED TO RACE, GENDER, AND SEXUALITY

bisexual: A person whose sexual orientation is based on attraction toward both genders; the identity developed based on these attractions.

bullying: Unwanted and often aggressive behavior involving real or perceived imbalance of power; such behavior is typically repeated over time or has the potential to be repeated.

cisgender: An individual who experiences his or her own gender as matching the sex assigned at birth; often abbreviated as "cis."

drag: Clothing worn by a person that is opposite his or her gender identity.

gay: A person whose sexual orientation is based on attraction toward that person's own gender; the identity developed based on these attractions. Gay is typically a term used by men, but some women also identify as gay.

gender: A socially constructed identity most often determined by one's biological sex.

gender conforming: Having traits and identities that adhere to gender-role expectations.

gender identity: A person's sense of identification as male, female, or another gender.

genderism: The ideology that reinforces the negative evaluation of gender nonconformity or a disconnect between sex and gender.

gender nonconforming: Having traits and identities that do not adhere to gender-role expectations.

gender presentation: The gender others perceive and assign to an individual based on dress, looks, and actions.

gender-role expectations: Assumptions that individuals will dress, act, speak, or believe in ways that conform to cultural norms associated with the sex assigned at birth.

gender roles: Expectations defined by societies and cultures about appropriate behaviors, norms, and values for women and men based on their gender.

gender variance: A behavior, style of dress, action, or identity that does not adhere to standard ideas of what it means to be a woman or man.

genderqueer: A self-descriptor for people whose internal sense and external expression of gender transgresses or challenges or moves beyond categorizations such as male and female and who live against culturally assigned norms of the male/female gender binary.

hate crime: Criminal act when the victim is targeted based on actual or perceived race, color, religion, national origin, ethnicity, disability, sexual orientation, gender, or gender identity.

hegemony: Dominance of one privileged social group over other social groups.

heteronormative: Condition that exists when attitudes, behaviors, and practices reflect the belief that heterosexuality is normative and that anything outside of heterosexuality is abnormal or deviant.

heterosexism: Negative attitudes, behaviors, and beliefs held by heterosexuals about nonheterosexual people and the discrimination that occurs as a result of such attitudes, behaviors, and beliefs.

homophobia: Emotional disgust or fear of homosexual people; fear of nonheterosexual people.

institutional discrimination: Unfair and discriminatory indirect treatment of an individual embedded in the procedures, laws, policies, or objectives of systems and organizations.

institutional racism: Any system of inequality based on race; unfair and discriminatory indirect treatment of an individual based on race and embedded in the procedures, laws, policies, or objectives of systems and organizations.

internalized homophobia: An aversion to one's own homosexual orientation as the result of accepting the heteronormative reality of oppressors and its standards, values, and beliefs.

internalized racism: An aversion to one's own racial/ethnic heritage as the result of accepting the racial reality of oppressors and its standards, values, and beliefs.

interpersonal discrimination: Unfair treatment between two or more individuals based on prejudices or stereotypes.

intersectional identities: The combination of individuals' multiple social groups and the identification, experiences, and worldviews that result from this combination.

intersex: People whose physical, hormonal, or chromosomal sex characteristics at birth do not fit neatly into the categories of either male or female but are ambiguous at birth.

lesbian: A woman whose sexual orientation is based on attraction toward her own gender; the identity developed based on these attractions.

LGBT: Acronym used to describe lesbian, gay, bisexual, and transgender people. Oftentimes, Q is added (LGBTQ) to include queer or questioning people.

misogyny: Dislike of or ingrained prejudice against women.

modern heterosexism: A system in which society marginalizes same-sex-oriented people while celebrating heterosexual people.

monoracism: A system of inequality and prejudice toward persons who do not fit into monoracial (single racial) identity categories or who embody multiple racial identities.

new racism: A form of both institutional and interpersonal racism that is systemic, underhanded, and often microaggressive in form; also called *modern racism*.

old racism: Prejudice against persons of color supposedly based on biological and essentialized differences between races.

patriarchy: A system in which men hold power and women are largely excluded from power.

person of color: A term used primarily in the United States to describe an individual who is not white.

queer: Originally used as an antigay slur stemming from the word's use to describe something odd, transgressive, strange, or eccentric. Subversively used as an umbrella term for all individuals who are not heterosexual or cisgender.

queering/to queer: Used as a verb, this term can indicate the intention to challenge the categories that we use to describe gender and sexuality. This act of thinking is often employed at times and places where we assume that certain categories of sexuality and gender are fixed and given in nature rather than socially constructed through the language and discourse. Thus "to queer" something might mean that one is questioning the assumptions, pushing the boundaries, and challenging normativity embedded in commonsensical understandings of the thing being "queered"—especially inasmuch as the thing being queered contributes to upholding rigid, fixed, and oppressive discourses on sexuality and gender.

questioning: Used to refer to individuals who are unsure of their sexual orientation or gender identity and cannot strictly label themselves as either heterosexual or cisgender. The *Q* in *LGBTQ* can stand for *questioning* or *queer*.

race-related fatigue: Exhaustion that results from receiving constant insults, invalidations, and hassles related to one's race.

racial mistrust: Defensiveness whereby white people are perceived as potential enemies unless they prove otherwise. Racial mistrust is often a result of race-related fatigue and/or race-related trauma.

racism: Prejudice and discrimination based on the perceived biological differences between people based on race.

sexism: Prejudice or discrimination based on sex, most often against women.

sexual identity: An individual's self-identification in terms of sexual and affectional orientation and experience and attraction; sometimes used interchangeably with *sexual orientation*.

sexual orientation: An individual's sense of identity based on one's sexual attractions and behaviors expressing those attractions.

targets: Those who are on the receiving end of microaggressive communications.

transgender: An umbrella term used to describe any individual who does not identify with the sex assigned at birth and/or who feels that such a gendered assignment is incorrect or incomplete. Transgender persons who choose to undergo a gender reassignment process—though importantly, not all do—may be described in the literature as MTF (male-to-female) or FTM (female-to-male) or, alternatively, transwoman and transman respectively.

transphobia: An emotional disgust or fear of individuals who do not conform to society's gender expectations; a fear of transgender people.

vicarious traumatization: The concept that people within oppressed social groups can experience degrees of psychological distress when a member of their same oppressed group is victimized.

white privilege: Privileges existing in predominantly white societies that benefit white people beyond what is regularly experienced by persons of color in the same society.

worldview: Collection of beliefs and perspectives from which one interprets and understands the world based on one's cultural identity, background, and life experience.